TEACHERS

Models of Excellence in Today's Classroom

JOYCE NESKER SIMMONS

WALTER PITMAN

Pembroke Publishers Limited

This book is dedicated to
the reader's teacher of the year.

© 1994 Pembroke Publishers
   538 Hood Road
   Markham, Ontario L3R 3K9

Canadian Cataloguing in Publication Data

Simmons, Joyce Nesker, 1941-
   Teachers: models of excellence in today's classroom

ISBN 1-55138-037-4

1. Teaching.
I. Pitman, Walter. II. Title.

LB1025.3.555 1994   371.1'02   C94-931827-2

Editor: David Kilgour
Design: John Zehethofer
Typesetting: Jay Tee Graphics Ltd.

This book was produced with the generous assistance of the government of Ontario through the Ministry of Culture, Tourism and Recreation.

Printed and bound in Canada by Webcom
9 8 7 6 5 4 3 2

Contents

Foreword

In recent years, teaching, as a profession, has fallen from public grace. The teacher has become everyone's favorite scapegoat for the ills of education.

Yet there is a world of difference between teaching and education. Education is the whole machine — the nuts, the bolts, the cogs, the wheels, the people and the product. It includes the problems of politics and the foibles of philosophy.

Teachers are the people who run the schools. They are the ants in the colony, workers who determine the quality of the daily life of each child in their care.

In the process of education, there can be no doubt — the teacher is the most important variable. A good teacher can make the difference between success and failure, between academic achievement and learning breakdown, between a university degree and the drop-out syndrome.

To the credit of the profession, many teachers do still make that critical difference despite changing agendas and increasingly uncertain demands. And the public bears witness to the far-reaching effects of their commitment.

As proof we offer the testimonials to top teachers that form the basis of this book. The information on teaching excellence that follows was amassed from first-hand reports by students, parents and colleagues submitted to the *Toronto Sun*, a newspaper which has conducted an annual "Teacher of the Year" contest since 1985.

As is well known, people too rarely go to the trouble to express praise; action is most easily triggered by anger or complaint. Moreover, a letter of nomination does not rest on a mere vote of support, an "X" in the ballot box. To nominate someone as a Teacher of the Year requires a major commitment of time and thought: a nominator must undertake the compilation of facts and in-depth character analysis, all expressed in a well-written, attention-grabbing letter. Who has the time? The interest? The motivation? Who, indeed!

The first Teacher of the Year contest was initiated quietly with a simple request in the educational advice column of the *Toronto Sun* written each week by Joyce Nesker Simmons:

> Do you know a good teacher? Is there some-
> one who has made a major contribution to
> your education? Can you think of a teacher
> who has been significant in your life? Please
> write and describe this person. Your
> nominating letter can take any form and
> include any type of information.

Sadly, it should be noted that the response in the field to this first notice was guarded. Most school administrators refused to take part. They excused themselves with reasons such as, "I don't believe in contests," or, "All my teachers are competent." The recognition of excellence was seen as an offensive rank order-ing with nothing for the profession to gain and much to lose. Teachers have always cherished the view that theirs is a profes-sion that eschews the obsessive preoccupation with competitive values which is so much a part of the private sector. In most cases, there are no remunerative rewards for being perceived as "first-class," as opposed to being just a "good" teacher. Teachers do not necessarily rise to become higher-paid principals and superintendents because they are able instructors. Indeed, if that happens it occasions criticism of the schools, because fine teachers are lost to the classroom and sink into the quagmire of "administration." In addition, professional teachers' organiza-tions have treated with utmost caution all proposals for rewarding outstanding teachers with special increments. In short, the ideal of great teachers working only to ensure the learning of students, with no thought of reward or recognition, is the Hippocratic oath that drives the teaching profession. An unrestrained and uncon-trolled Teacher of the Year contest could be a breech in the armor of perceived integrity and recognized service to humankind which has impelled the profession to excellence in performance for so very long.

In spite of hesitation on the part of teachers, however, the public was much more responsive and positive. Hundreds of letters arrived at Simmons' desk from all over Ontario, most coming from the Golden Horseshoe around Toronto, an area which represents the major circulation reach of the *Sun*. Then, of course, judges had to be found whose experience of the field was broad and whose integrity was beyond question.

The first year produced a single Teacher of the Year, Elaine Vine, a teacher whose accomplishments are recorded later in this volume. The prize that year was merely accolades from students, colleagues and administrators. They spread a red carpet through the school in the form of construction paper and the principal gave her a bouquet of flowers. A simple plaque and her photograph in the paper followed. Yet that recognition was valued by Elaine Vine as the highlight of her personal life and career when she said,

> I've never been engaged, I've never been
> married; you've finally given me something
> my mother can brag about.

In 1986, in addition to the plaque, there was a dinner for the winner and a few friends given by an interested trustee.

As the contest has grown, the winners have received the inevitable plaque — but a more formal presentation at the Ontario Institute for Studies in Education has emerged as the central event at which hundreds of friends, students and colleagues join in an afternoon of celebration. In the late '80s, the winning teachers were honored, first at a football game, then at a Blue Jays baseball game in the SkyDome, with public introductions and responses from a crowd waiting for the game to commence. No handsome cheque. No medals or medallions. No lavish gifts of cars or exotic holiday trips. Just the reward of knowing their superior performance as professionals has been recognized.

With time, the attitude of school administration and professional organizations changed to complete cooperation and active involvement in encouraging nominations. Now, each year, thousands of teachers are nominated, many by their colleagues. More than 10,000 teachers in all have been nominated and while they share a common time and place, the qualities they represent are both timeless and without boundaries.

One thing has become obvious from the thousands of letters that attest to the popularity of the Teachers of the Year. Each of us has had, in our school lives, a special teacher. And, the impact of such a teacher can be extraordinary.

Consider these words, for example, written about a Grade 8 teacher on reflection after eighteen years.

> He taught us more than academic subjects. He taught us bravery. When we were all crying hysterically in the schoolyard after a bomb threat, he played his guitar and sang to us to calm us. He taught us to respect ourselves and others. He had great hopes for all of us and all that we could become. He let us know when we had disappointed him, and we felt regret. He told us when he was proud of us and we felt pride and joy. He expected the best from us and very often he got it.

We hope that by presenting profiles of teachers like this and highlighting their common characteristics, our book will offer direction to a profession now in flux, for never have teachers felt so inadequate, never has morale in the schools been so palpably low, never has the esteem of the public been so wanting.

Schooling has always had a very defined role expressed in many different ways — that of putting young people in contact with the information they must have to cope with their lives in society, or that of instructing them in the ways they can find that information. The public has always emphasized the importance of teaching children basic skills — numeracy, the literacies of language, science and technology, the excitement of social, economic and artistic exploration, and something of the value system which is accepted by our society at large.

There has always been a clear connection between schools, marketable skills and knowledge, and jobs. But our society does not seem capable of producing jobs, or ''good work,'' for its graduating students. And the schools are blamed both for the unemployed graduate and the economic ills that beset the country and thereby erode our hopes for the good life.

Also, schools are expected to reflect the ethical and behavioral standards of the community. But what if that community is so diverse and expectations are so conflicting that the classroom can provide only a mélange of multicultural expression rather than a clear philosophical position?

Never before have violence and the classroom been associated as a problem seeking a solution. But in certain settings teachers find themselves and their students at risk every day of their lives.

All these are just some of the problems facing today's teachers. The picture of a classroom with a blackboard, the teacher at the front of the room and a collection of eager, excited learners with an essential homogeneity that ensures collective learning is a nostalgic illusion. Today it is individual needs and the expectation of tailored response that must capture the attention of the successful teacher. A roomful of electronic equipment with which the students often seem more at home than the teacher represents a major challenge.

The models of excellence profiled in this book, all winners of the Teacher of the Year contest, set the standards so that others can learn and grow by exposure to positve, meaningful examples. After all, isn't that the goal of effective teaching?

CHAPTER 1

Six Standards of Success

For the record, we are both teachers. Over the years, we have gone in other directions, but we still define ourselves in terms of the work for which we qualified when we were barely old enough to vote.

We still spend time in schools, often in the classroom. No longer in regular active duty, we are there to observe and to discuss what we see later. During our visits, we are simply other faces in the crowd, and like the rest of the class our enjoyment of these sessions depends mainly on the competence and personality of the teacher in charge. Our book is written from this perspective — the view from the back of the room, so to speak.

Most people agree that there are certain characteristics that separate the ordinary teacher from the extraordinary. Many of these traits are "people skills" — the ability to communicate, to show warmth, to be considerate and consistent, to maintain a sense of humor, in total to enjoy and be enjoyed by all kinds of people: children, their families, colleagues.

Ironically, the most committed fans are often the students who barely register on the consciousness of either the class or the teacher — the quiet person in his or her own corner.

The following accolade, for example, was written by an adult as a tribute after the death of a favorite high school teacher; a teacher, like most, who will never share the retrospective expression of appreciation:

> My academic career is not littered with gold
> stars, framed report cards or cherished certifi-
> cates. I was definitely not the kid at the front

of the class waving his arm. I was more apt to be found huddled near the back, trying desperately not to make eye contact and avoiding certain embarrassment over being queried about my unfinished assignment.

My report cards could be found under dressers, buried in my sock drawer or conveniently "lost" in transit. Those long, agonizing waits for my parents to arrive home after a parent-teacher night were almost unbearable.

Through the luck of scheduling, the theatre arts class was bright and early every morning and I occasionally looked forward to it between a late breakfast and a rendezvous at the doughnut shop. When I did drop in, I was anchored at my usual post, trading guffaws with others who were less artistically inclined.

My fantasies of easy street were brought to an abrupt end one day as I lunged for the door. I was gently grabbed by the arm and quietly dragged back to my corner for a quiet consultation.

Upset that I would miss my daily euchre game, I was less than attentive at first. But what Mr. Reynolds said that morning still has an impact on me today.

He said that he needed me to do well. He said that I had the potential to do well not only in his class but in everything. He didn't lambaste me for my attitude. Instead he encouraged me not only to participate but to motivate my classmates as well.

Later that year, in preparation for our school play, he even prompted me to replace an ailing classmate in the role of the doctor in *The Miracle Worker*. (After one rehearsal, frantic calls were made and the original doctor was able to carry on under heavy medication. But that's show business.)

I was made business manager, hardly Conrad Black, but Mr. Reynolds was there every step of the way, encouraging me when things looked their worst and giving me a pat on the back when things turned around.

I'm not going to finish this letter by telling you that those few months of encouragement changed my entire attitude, like in an Andy Hardy movie. I am not the overnight success story that would be the perfect ending to this tale. I made my way through high school and four years of university and now have a job that I enjoy because of its challenge and my sense of dedication.

What Mr. Reynolds did was find that "switch." He showed me that I had the confidence to try anything. Like my brief fling with acting, I might not always succeed, but the satisfaction in just trying is sometimes fulfilling enough.

I have had teachers with varying degrees of dedication whose approaches to teaching are as different as night and day. With students like me I realize just how easy it would be to become frustrated and pessimistic. Yelling and reprimands may vent frustration, but would just drive students like me farther away.

When I attend seminars and conferences today, I still find myself gravitating to the rear of the class but at least now I'm raising my hand. Thank you, Mr. Reynolds, from the guy at the back of the class.

However, having passed the "nice guy" test, good teachers must also measure up to the yardsticks imposed by their professional community. They must, in the final analysis, be successful in imparting knowledge.

An examination of the teaching process is never easy. Like any other good relationship, that of successful teacher and pupil involves a certain quota of magic. But at its best this relationship means that teachers learn from students as much as students learn from teachers. Examples of this double flow of understanding form the basis of the following pages and, indeed, are the *raison d'être* of our book. The learning process is never one-sided.

Take, as model, the role of Lena Daley in the life of her favorite teacher, Brenda McKelvie. Lena never entered high school; cancer cut her life short. Yet, despite her youth, and in the midst of painful treatments, she took the time to be a nominator and thereby teach us all a huge lesson in understanding life in relation to the learning equation. She did it all by describing a winning Teacher of the Year and how the interaction affected her.

From this description and from the information provided by all the other submissions, we have analysed the winning characteristics of the thousands of teachers nominated as Teachers of the Year. The results of our analysis indicate that successful teaching rests on certain common key standards which, while not precisely measureable, serve as beacons illuminating the way to excellence. We have defined the good teacher as one who is:

1. FLEXIBLE:

Invariably in the learning process, someone is frustrated. Since the route to knowledge rarely follows a single direct path, both teachers and students must continually confront change. Usually the task befalls the student, because teachers tend to lead and students to follow a prepared, non-deviating program. A good teacher, however, is able to abandon short-term goals on any day, in any lesson, for any child. Only then can significant learning goals be kept clearly in sight.

2. INTERESTING:

Computers have become popular in education for one key reason: they motivate students. Teachers should take note. Granted, keeping an audience in the palm of your hand for six hours a day is no easy task. But then paying attention over an extended time to a dull teacher is even more demanding.

3. AVAILABLE:

The teaching day offers few spare moments. Nonetheless a good teacher, like a good parent, is there when needed and is always easy to approach. That capacity to appear concerned and caring about students at all times must be cultivated. There is no attribute which seems to inspire greater respect and admiration from students and their parents.

4. INFORMED:

The name of the game is education, yet teachers can be the worst proponents of literacy and learning. A good teacher demonstrates by example the values of scholarship and the benefits of clear written expression. This means more than having acquired the academic levels that the law requires of all applicants to faculties of education. It means possessing the curious, questioning mind of an adult learner who never ceases to explore the frontiers of knowledge.

5. ACCOUNTABLE:

Report cards and interviews are often moments of truth. Then parents and students know whether the teacher is aware of herself or himself as a main feature of the learning environment. A teacher who states, "Matthew can't read," "Amy does not complete her work," or "Timmy is bugging the other children," without seeking explanations and suggesting changes, is shirking responsibility.

6. RELEVANT:

Today's troubled economy means a difficult job market. From parents to children, families share uncertainty about the future, and this uncertainty is compounded by the fact that education *per se* is no longer a ticket to success. A teacher who can translate school learning into meaning in the world outside the classroom walls has learned the language of relevance and is addressing the public's expectations for the 21st century.

In the following chapters profiles of top teachers are offered to illustrate these six standards, and these profiles are supported by dynamic descriptions of professional competence as offered by the teachers' most loyal fans.

There will be those who will consider these measures of achievement beyond all rational expectation for the average classroom teacher who seeks to do a creditable job day by day. But the teachers whose success has been chronicled in this small volume are not superhuman. They have all the frailties of humankind. They may be caught in webs of family responsibility, ill health, overwork — essentially the devastating personal circumstances that sometimes beset us all.

Although we have attempted to focus on the most dramatic attributes of particular teachers, we are aware that every "winner" exudes a capacity to work up to a high level for each standard we have identified. These are multi-dimensional people who can be interesting, accountable, available, informed, relevant and flexible. They may exhibit seemingly overwhelming capabilities in one area of our pursuit of excellence — but they rise to extraordinary heights in every aspect of their performance.

This may indeed be the lesson for all who seek the role of teacher, either in the formal setting of the public school or in the varied settings for learning in the private industrial and commercial or the voluntary sectors of our society. We all have certain strengths that can be honed and polished. These give us the confidence to teach anything. Knowing these capacities allows us to design our own style of teaching and to choreograph our own professional behavior. It also gives us the confidence to assess and reasses our performance day by day. It signals to us areas of weakness that need to be "shored up."

Teaching has tended to be a lonely profession. But of late, strategies for voluntary mentoring of new teachers and genuine partnering of experienced teachers based on mutual respect but dependent as well on honest critical analysis, have expanded the opportunities for teachers to collaborate with colleagues in their search for improved performance. This is to be applauded and emulated. Continuous self-examination and the acceptance of constant appraisal from colleagues together represent the highest form of professional accountability.

Yet we must ask for more. More than most professions, teaching is about the future. The children in our classrooms will likely live through political and socio-economic crises that we have not faced. But we have the responsibility of providing them with the tools to overcome these crises and the structure of knowledge on which to build anew.

As an example, we are now aware that the opportunities for continuing lifelong employment may not be what they once were. Part-time jobs, shared jobs, periodic unemployment will be a part of the pattern of society in the 21st century. Students who have learned the lessons of increased self-reliance, who have learned to think creatively, who have developed self-confidence and flexibility will be more able to cope with the shifting sands of an unstable economy.

Young people who have a sense of worth that extends beyond their paying jobs to include contributions to the voluntary sectors which support a humane community and the artistic and recreational activities which give joy and self-fulfilment, will have been well prepared for that future.

Teachers who count have that sense of the future which will help them empower students who will no longer have the expectations of the affluent but unrealistic latter half of the 20th century. It may be an uncertain, difficult future, but it is also rife with possibilities, possibilities we must help our students realize.

CHAPTER 2

The Flexible Teacher

Learning is never static; by definition, it is about change. And like the process, learners are constantly evolving, with needs and interests that can barely be declared before they change.

To be successful, a teacher must accept this challenge of change. No timetable, no daily plan, no guidebook can take precedence over the ever-evolving, ever-developing dynamics of learning.

For a teacher, the capacity to shift gears, to recognize the individual needs of dozens of students in a classroom, to assess the adequacy and relevance to those students of the curriculum materials that are available, demands real flexibility.

Every day is a new experience for student and teacher alike. Every day presents a new challenge, that of nurturing a dynamic interaction that will enable students to learn skills and information they didn't know at sunrise, and one hopes that they will still be curious at sunset. The expectations of students and parents are so diverse and, in some cases, so unreasonable that it is a mystery that teachers turn up day after day to recreate this extraordinary magic.

For many teachers and students, on many days, the magic does not materialize. Students may come to school feeling angry or lonely. In some cases, such students will want to act out their frustrations on fellow inhabitants of the classroom — including the teacher. As well, teachers themselves have families and domestic problems that beset them as inexorably as they do any other human being, and the desire to unload their frustrations on a captive audience can be hard to resist. One of the surprising common traits of the great teachers identified in this volume is their ability to put aside their own "crosses to bear." Perhaps it is through coping with their personal daily pressures that they come to realize the essential quality of flexibility that must be the characteristic of a splendid teacher.

Ernest Kuechmeister

For much of his career in education, Ernie Kuechmeister has been a principal, but he doesn't play the part of king of the castle. On the contrary, Ernie Kuechmeister is a dedicated, front-line educator who still lives in classrooms and regularly does yard duty.

Ernie began teaching in a sparsely populated, northern mining community and then moved first to one, then to another developed area, both similar in their suburban yet cosmopolitan settings.

For the last twenty-five years of his career, he has remained with the same large school board taking on a range of challenges in elementary education, including many years working with severely disabled children.

Within a wide range of schools, Ernie has always maintained an open-door policy. The principal's office is a familiar and welcoming place with home baking frequently prepared by Ernie's wife, Moni, and a friendly shoulder to lean on offered by the man many students call "cookie monster."

This warm, supportive, flexible principal will often abandon his regular schedule to play chess with a child who needs a little extra time or attention. He is also noted for his availability in the classroom or for yard duty and for meeting student personal needs as they arise, whether they be for food, clothing, money or emotional care. His focus, he says, is mental health, and in both school and community he is always ready to support this area of children's well-being.

He says,

> Mental health is a major problem to society
> and people avoid it because they find it
> threatening. I see children who carry the scars
> of mental illness and seeing the impact I look
> to help out.

As part of helping out, Ernie Kuechmeister envisions his students' lives far beyond the walls of the school. He is always ready to relieve stress or find alternative remedies for life's ills.

In all ways flexible, Ernie and his wife became parents late in life. Their commitment to living, learning and education as change are best exemplified in this new personal venture which happened when a member of Ernie's staff became ill with cancer. As the disease progressed, her caring principal was supportive and available as needed. When faced with death she asked him to care for her two young adolescents. They had no other family. She died in peace knowing that her children had found a new home with the Kuechmeisters who had been childless until then.

One of the greatest surprises in the field of education is the fact that so many of the best teachers find their way into administration. Better remuneration and new challenges lure many to become vice-principals, principals, consultants, superintendents — the list of out-of-classroom positions is endless. In the belt-tightening future, it may be that there will be fewer middle management positions, and that may solve in part the problem of the serious loss of thousands of fine teachers from the classroom. But another solution would be the role of administrators like Ernie Kuechmeister who are dedicated to spending a considerable amount of time and energy with children in learning activities. It means re-defining the role of educational administration. It means changing the reward system in schools. It means getting the priorities of school boards and schools right. All of this demands flexibility.

Elaine Vine

In our image of the traditional classroom, students arrive at 9:00 a.m. and leave seven hours later at 4:00 p.m. It is assumed that for the years of childhood and adolescence, school is the major focus of their lives.

However, there are young people of school age who have exhibited talent and commitment outside the classroom. Obviously, sports attract men and women to careers that begin with childhood dreams, move on to countless hours of practice and ultimately lead to employment that may last but a few years beyond reaching adulthood. In some cases, it is not a matter of preparing for a job at all, but the opportunity of achieving the glory of an Olympic medal in a sport that offers no commercial return. In the arts, the pressure to achieve heights of excellence as a musician or a dancer can start at an early age. In these cases school can seem a barrier to achievement that really matters to the youthful mind and spirit.

On the other hand, in both arts and athletics, many may be called, but few are chosen. Even those chosen may have only a few years to earn a living in a physically punishing enterprise until they find themselves unemployed and untrained in a demanding labor market.

The teacher who has the flexibility along with a myriad other capacities to deal with such students deserves to be a Teacher of the Year. Just such a teacher is Elaine Vine.

Elaine directs an alternative secondary school program called "Interact" for students who can give minimal time and attention to their formal education. Yet she is able to adjust her response to the needs of each student in such a way that their time in the classroom has quality and relevance. It is her task to convince each student that what she teaches may not enhance their performance on the ice, the gym floor or the stage but in the long run may enhance their lives and their capacity to achieve a long-term livelihood.

Only with great flexibility can a teacher make school accommodate students with individual training programs in the arts or sports, students who are not able to guarantee regular attendance or consistent performance of assignments. Elaine Vine does this and at the same time as meeting changing schedules and workloads develops individualized programs which can compete dramatically with the student's first love, natural talent and public recognition.

As her nominee put it so succinctly:

> How is this accomplished? It is done by Elaine
> and her staff who provide a nurturing
> learning environment, exacting standards,
> genuine support and pride in earned
> accomplishment.

Perhaps Elaine Vine is particularly sensitive to the changing circumstances that affect the lives of all of us. For some years, she taught in an elementary school and developed a literature-based drama curriculum that, in the words of an admirer, "encouraged the most reluctant learner to experience self-confidence, self-worth and the joy of learning."

From that experience she went on to the "Interact" program and teaching in secondary school. Her transformation reminds one that teachers may pursue many careers within the teaching framework, moving from one kind of school to another, from a traditional school program to an experimental situation, from lower grades to higher. The good teacher carries all her experiences with her, enriching her performance at each stage with wisdom gathered before, as does Elaine Vine. Moving from a focus on a drama curriculum to a program for special students concentrating on their athletic or performing skills is an enormous leap indeed.

Each transition takes a toll as well. A flexible teacher must often be prepared to pay the price of extra hours of listening and learning, waiting and preparing, always in the wings, so to speak. This is no nine-to-five job, as Elaine's nominator pointed out:

> I acknowledge that individuals who pioneer a
> new concept or program have additional
> responsibilities to ensure success, especially in
> a forum such as public education. I admire
> Elaine's ability to achieve such success,
> recognizing at the same time that this ability is
> something Elaine never takes for granted.
> Hard work-hours of dedicated preparation, of
> reaching out to students and of service to
> colleagues — complement her natural talents.

Indeed there is a price to pay once the teacher leaves the well-trodden path to venture into the innnovative. Elaine Vine has created a role for education that has allowed the school's schedule to accommodate the students' schedules so that her fortunate few can focus on future goals and not leave their present needs behind.

What is the ultimate reason for Elaine Vine's success? A parent comments:

Above all, Elaine respects the student and believes wholeheartedly in the potential of every learner to achieve success. Her students acquire a lesson for a lifetime — a belief in themselves.

And what of our distorted definiton of the flexible teacher as weak and vacillating in character? Teachers on the fringe find that they must defend their roles and practices every day of the week. In their professional lives, the term "flexible" becomes a synonym for "courage."

As the parent who nominated Elaine Vine observes about this teacher who must continually do battle for her students' special schedules as a part of her regular duties:

Some would call her outspoken, others outrageous, but everyone calls her the best.

A flexible teacher like Elaine recognizes that learning is a continuing lifelong activity. While recognizing the need to ensure that certain basic skills are emphasized at appropriate points in a student's life, each one pursues those areas that seem relevant and significant. "Interact" is a lesson in adjusting teaching and learning to the interests of the learner, rather than imposing the inexorable flow of the curriculum.

Dolores Fraser

Dolores Fraser has always been a very busy woman. Born in the tourist area of Niagara Falls, she married, moved to the big city, had three children and taught school.

She has been at her current school since it opened twenty-six years ago. For the past number of years, she has taught Junior Kindergarten in the morning and been the school's librarian for the rest of the day. She is also involved with the school's chess club, badminton, track and field, and arts festival.

Her school principal says about her:

What is so special about this teacher? Well, first of all, there is her boundless energy. For a woman of 50+ (she will never tell her age) she leaps around that classroom with those young tykes, and runs, hops, skips and jumps like them — and yet she has time to attend to all their needs. In the library it is not simply a question of signing out books; she has to know what project the children are engaged in, whether it is well prepared, if they need more resources, how she can help.

More than anything, though, her devotion to the school and children endear her to all. At 8:00 a.m. she will be at school to work with the chess club. After school she will remain behind to supervise the older students at badminton. On top of this she still finds time to work on many other school projects; Hallowe'en, the Christmas concert, the arts festival.

To many people in our community this school is Dolores Fraser. It is her spirit of tireless work that is communicated to students and staff alike. To children, staff and parents, Mrs. Fraser is a constant. She has been here from the first day. In that time she has been an exemplar of discipline, of hard work and of dedication to children.

Along the way Ms. Fraser raised her own three children, who all completed their university degrees, and she now is a very proud grandmother.

A model for us all, Dolores Fraser is a successful teacher both at home and at school. She is always open to challenge and forever available to the learning needs of each child in her care. And, after all, following the path of each learner demands the flexible approach since learning rarely proceeds en route without detour.

A flexible teacher is one who can abandon predetermined courses and not care too much about daily plans.

As the secretary at Dolores Fraser's school says:

If the definition of a good teacher is one who

is committed to the children's needs, then
Dolores is a good teacher. If the definition of a
great teacher is one who loves the children
and generously serves their needs, then
Dolores is a great teacher. But if the definition
of an outstanding teacher is an educator who
is totally pledged to children, a tutor who
loves and cherishes each child's uniqueness, a
guide who respects and appreciates the
difficulties and dreams in a child's egocentric
world, a coach who esteems the effortless
grace of the inherent athlete as well as the
awkward struggles of the naturally unwieldy,
then Dolores Fraser is indeed an extraordinary
teacher.

Within a school, no job demands more flexibility than that of
the librarian. This person must constantly be on call for a range
of demands and subject matter often foreign to basic personal
knowledge.

A teaching colleague found out just how important these
strengths were when she personally needed Dolores Fraser's support as a resource person.

She is dedicated to helping out in her capacity
as teacher-librarian. Her expert knowledge of
our school library and other resources are
invaluable to our staff members. Recently I
had an assignment for my librarian's course
and Dolores almost instantly was able to
retrieve excellent materials for me.

As a teacher-librarian she will team-teach a
unit with your class. Last year she taught
Cinquaine poetry to my grade five. They were
hooked on writing that type of poetry and so
was I.

Apply this flexible approach to the classroom, especially in the
very early years, and you have the list of winning characteristics of a child-centred teacher listed by one of her Junior Kindergarten students:

1. Mrs. Fraser is very helpful.
2. Mrs. Fraser reads stories to us.
3. Mrs. Fraser never gets mad.
4. Mrs. Fraser is kind.
5. Mrs. Fraser likes kids.
6. Mrs. Fraser plays chess.
7. Mrs. Fraser takes lots of sports.
8. Mrs. Fraser is pretty.
9. Mrs. Fraser is like a mother to us.
10. Mrs. Fraser shares her books.
11. Mrs. Fraser is fun to be with.
12. Mrs. Fraser is very, very nice.
13. We like her books.
14. She lets people use the library.
15. Mrs. Fraser helps everybody.
16. Mrs. Fraser is willing.
17. When people lose one of her books, she is still not mad.

One of the stresses of teaching that receives little attention is the enormous drain of physical and psychic energy it takes every day. Interacting over six hours in a classroom with thirty children, each on his or her own learning journey, each carrying a full knapsack of personal treasures and problems, is exhausting. Even more daunting is the experience of the secondary schoolteacher who must meet a couple of hundred students over a single day, for shorter periods of time admittedly, but nonetheless each child expects a totally dedicated and energetic response to learning needs.

It says something about the importance all teachers should give to their own physical and mental well-being. We hear so much about the burn-out of teachers, and only a more supportive system can mitigate this situation. But teachers must take time to ensure that their health and mental well-being are not in jeopardy. Otherwise they and their students will be the losers.

Alan Kingston

Al Kingston has re-entered the teaching profession for a second time around. After taking early retirement a couple of years ago, he set out to operate a trailer park in Northern Ontario. However, a few short months after his retirement, his youngest daughter, a first-year university student, became ill with acute viral encephalitis. Al stayed by her side throughout a three-month-long coma and, despite a very pessimistic prognosis, he began the most difficult teaching task of his life: reteaching his daughter how to talk, walk and ultimately return to normal life.

The youngest member of the Kingston family has astonished doctors and rehabilitation specialists, thanks to the excellent personal teaching she received. Amazingly, she has returned to school. And so has Dad. Al Kingston is teaching science and physical education this year at a secondary school after many years of teaching history and geography, and he is proving by example that effort, commitment and caring are sure to pay off when backed by buoyancy.

Al Kingston was nominated as Teacher of the Year by his middle daughter, who grew up accutely aware of her father's all-inclusive commitment to teaching. How could she not be?

She remembers her father leaving the house before dawn most days to be at the rink or the field before the team arrived so that he could supervise hockey or football practices; she remembers how late he stayed at school each day to provide extra help to students; she remembers the constant after-hour telephone calls and visits from students who needed more than the school day had to offer.

And she remembers weekends also filled with a devotion to education, this time in the form of volunteer work with children with disabilities.

But these are distant memories. Most current in her mind is her father as teacher, in his finest hour, the midst of a medical crisis, refusing to accept heartbreak and defeat as he persisted in the rehabilitation of her ill sister.

To describe this excellent teacher, friend and father, she wrote:

> This man gave of himself totally to all the students he taught and many of his former students, now adults, have kept in touch with him, to thank him for his efforts, support and understanding that he gave them. Many of these people I have spoken with myself say it was this teacher Al Kingston that they

remember from high school and that his teaching has left a lasting impression with them they will never forget. With the educational system constantly changing with the times, this teacher has adapted with an open mind and heart all the challenges it puts forth. Interesting students from all walks of life, e.g., teenagers coming from broken homes, physically and emotionally abused children, immigrants that can speak only minimal English, racial gangs, drug and alcohol addicted teens, are only a few challenges he has to deal with everyday. I remember him expressing sincere concern for his students' welfare and success in their studies. He often made a point to stay late to give extra instruction and attention to the pupils who spoke little English, in order for them to cope and adapt better in his regular classroom and in their new environment. He also mentioned that it is not uncommon for an adolescent boy to request a little "fatherly" advice from him because they are being raised solely by their mother. On a regular basis he encounters racial conflicts with student gangs and he tries to help them understand the disagreeable consequences of some of their actions through counselling and proper discipline. In every student he teaches, he encourages them to think for themselves and develop solid morals and values any parent would be proud of. One of the best sayings he relayed to all his guests at his January 1990 retirement party was, "No matter what circumstances arise in your life, just be there and adjust. By just being there, you will be, at the least of your efforts, attempting to conquer and master any challenge in life."

Al Kingston accepted the greatest challenge of all, that of taking responsibility for his own daughter's education in the most difficult of circumstances. There is a lesson in this for every teacher. Determine how to treat each student as if you held the ultimate responsibility of being their parent. It may seem a staggering burden. And yet, is this not what we hope for each young person, that they will meet and learn from a teacher who will be at some level a surrogate parent, a deeply caring person, able to adjust to that child's immediate learning needs? Perhaps an unfair expectation of teachers, but also, perhaps, an admirable objective.

Barbara MacLellan

Barbara MacLellan has had a remarkably varied teaching career that spans three provinces and three decades. She grew up and began teaching in New Brunswick, married, and then taught in Quebec before moving to Ontario, where she has worked in both private and public systems, teaching both elementary and secondary grades.

Since 1976, Barbara has been with the Etobicoke Board of Education, first at Richview Collegiate and then at Lakeshore Collegiate. She is currently teaching females aged eighteen to twenty-one in a prison setting, at a west end detention centre. Her job is to kindle an interest in learning and a trust in formal education, in students for whom the term "drop-out" takes on new significance.

The re-entry to society of these troubled women depends on the success of the rehabilitation process and the formal education component of that process is Barbara MacLellan's job.

She was nominated as Teacher of the Year by an inmate at the detention centre who had been a teacher in Michigan before her imprisonment and thus was able to work as a classroom assistant while at the Metro Toronto West Detention Centre.

The inmate wrote:

> The dictionary defines the word "teacher" as
> one who instructs or teaches but Barb
> MacLellan does far more than just instruct or
> teach these young women in need. She is a
> combination teacher, mother, confidante and
> self-esteem builder.

To work within a prison setting does, indeed, demand a very special type of flexibility. A program must be developed, yet the teacher must work without clear commitment from the pupils. Students in detention centres are inmates first and foremost so that educators must accept that time frames vary, meetings interrupt programs, and rules and regulations are a regular way of life.

Educational success in such an atmosphere rests with a teacher who can commit to short-term goals yet register forever with her students.

As Barbara's nominator wrote:

> Not only does she encourage their learning, but she takes a personal interest in every student's welfare. I have been fortunate enough to be one of these women who have experienced this interest, not as a student but as a teaching assistant in the school. For five months I have worked alongside of her and she has been a stabilizing influence on me during a time of personal turmoil, as well as being an excellent role model for teaching.
>
> A large number of these students have very little formal education and very short attention spans. It takes a great deal of patience and ingenuity to encourage them to do their school work. Besides the usual subjects of math or English, there is also incorporated into this program a knowledge of computers, sewing and knitting. This diversity seems to keep the program in a positive mode. Mrs. McLellan uses her excellent interpersonal skills to work with women on an individual basis. The results have been that many women leave with certificates of credit in math and English, a stronger feeling of self-worth and a desire to continue their education in the community.
>
> It takes a special kind of person to brave coming into a prison atmosphere to encourage learning and this teacher is the most "special" kind of person. Therefore, I would like to see her get some recognition for her dedication and caring regarding educating women in prison.

SUMMARY

Learning means change.

On a constant basis, a student must confront demands that require evolution of thought and understanding if skills development is to occur. In this regard, the learner is the biggest risk-taker of all.

To support the precarious learning process, the teacher, too, must take chances and be ever-alert to new ways of supporting students on the treacherous route to knowledge.

Is this what you need? What do you want to know? How can you understand? What might make you feel better? Where do you want me to fit into the context of learning? These are the questions that the flexible teacher asks.

The models of excellence offered in this chapter are exceptional in their flexibility. Whether in the office, the library, the home, the hospital, the classroom or the prison, all are leaders who know how and when to follow lessons in adaptability that should be basic to our definition of effective teaching.

CHAPTER 3

The Interesting Teacher

There can be no doubt: teaching in schools has been undermined by the effects of hard-sell entertainment. Video games, television and stereophonic sound have all had a major impact on learning, an impact we ignore at our peril.

Our children are no longer innocents. Their interest has been grabbed, their eyes, ears and minds mesmerized by advertising and programming experts. Those who know how to reach an audience have got our children's attention. For a teacher, *Sesame Street* is a tough act to follow.

For these reasons, a good teacher must be wise in the ways of sparking interest. The school's hold on knowledge has been challenged, and it is no longer exclusive. Educators must now compete with a variety of learning frontiers and a wealth of teaching formats. This may well be for the best, but it requires extra effort on our part. A good teacher in today's world must try to be as good as programs that win awards and products that command high price tags.

The message here is simple.

Take chances! Express yourself!
You too can light a learning fuse!

Ted Potochniak

Ted Potochniak is a storyteller. He not only tells tales, his words weave the fabric of dreams.

Just mention his name to any student, from Kindergarten to

Grade 8, from any school he has taught in for the past thirty years, and the immediate response will include a wistful look and a memory of a favorite yarn about dragons, giants or wizards.

No one talks in a room when Ted Potochniak tells a story. The interest of the class is complete. There is no distraction great enough to compete with the joy of listening to "Mr. P."

Ted Potochniak is also an athlete. When still in high school himself, he signed a football contract and went on to play professional ball until injuries sidelined him and he turned to teaching. Nowadays, he plays only school sports, but he plays them daily — football, baseball, floor hockey — with both male and female students, usually devoting his lunch hour and time after school to coaching.

The other major interest he shares with his students is his love of fishing, and his students are usually treated to several heavenly spring excursions with bait, hook and rod in hand and school left far behind.

But it is in the classroom that Ted Potochniak earns his top honors. His program is described by countless supporters among students, colleagues and parents as "enriching," "designed to draw out the best each student has to offer," "an atmosphere where students are encouraged to express themselves freely," "sensitive," and "out of this world."

As one student outlined in twenty points, Mr. P. is his favorite teacher because he is:

1. A very nice person
2. A very good fisherman
3. Takes time to help us
4. Very understanding
5. Very patient
6. A great athlete
7. A very smart person
8. A fantastic eater
9. Very funny
10. A great scientist
11. An amazing storyteller
12. Isn't picky (about messy desks)
13. In love with his students
14. Very interesting to listen to
15. Very fair (doesn't favor anybody)

16. Absolutely great at dishing out homework
17. Not a show-off
18. An absolutely great father
19. A great inspirer
20. A winner. A winner. A winner. A winner.
    A winner. A winner. A winner. A winner.
    A WINNER.

Since Ted Potochniak is comfortable with students of any age, he has taught every level of elementary school. One particularly difficult challenge was the three-year period he devoted to teaching an enrichment program and taking his fortunate students through all the junior grades.

Yet despite this remarkable workload, he kept his commitments in sports and storytelling for the entire school population, often combining the two specialties with surprising results for shy students who, before they could hesitate, took on new ventures and risks under the magic spell of Mr. P.

No wonder a fellow teacher who taught with him for many years says about him:

> He has sparked his students' interest in many
> diverse subject areas. He is an expert at
> encouraging his students to develop their
> interests in storytelling, art and science,
> as well as all the other subjects he teaches.
> He truly makes learning a joy for all.

Today's student knows from a very early age that life is a drama and its various phases can be approached in an exciting way. We live in the TV age and to compete, teachers must acquire the qualities of actors and the capacity to express themselves with dynamic intensity.

Leanne Iravanni

> I simply have to grab my thesaurus and look
> up the word "great" and I will find an entire
> list describing this superb lady.

So began a former student's description of a science teacher she also calls her "coach," "confidante," "counsellor" and "friend."

Leanne Iravanni is a small-town girl through and through. She grew up and went to school in the same rural community in which she now teaches. In fact, shortly after attending university and completing teacher training, she was hired for her first job by the vice-principal she had as a youngster. Leanne had come home.

As a teacher Leanne's enthusiasm has been termed "infectious" by her colleagues and she has interested the entire staff in some of the subjects raised in her science classes, mainly environmental issues and pollution control. She is relentless in working to promote a positive environmental ethic within the schoool and she is constantly organizing recycling programs. She also creates school assemblies with environmental themes and brings to them the concerns of the wider community, in which she serves in a broad network of committees.

The environmentalist movement was looked upon first as a passing phase, another bandwagon that teachers were invited to jump on. However, teachers like Leanne recognize that the environment will be one of the most important issues of the next century and that her students will likely spend most of their lives confronting it.

Courage and a sense of the future are essentials for teachers if they are to have the relentlessness in educating that is both justified and necessary. Leanne knows that her students will see their values challenged and their lifestyles changed as a result of the need to save the planet and she manages to inject these very serious issues into the lives of her students through enthusiastic example and personal commitment.

Her students describe this infectious enthusiasm when talking about her classes. One student remarked,

> Over the years, I have no doubt in my mind that Mrs. I.'s grade eleven advanced biology class had to have been the best class I have ever taken. Though we were forced to take hundreds of pages of notes, Mrs. I. always made the class exciting. By using common examples of everyday life, she managed to

explain the most difficult of terms to us. She
taught us as a team and soon enough we
began functioning as a team. We all felt bad
when someone did not do well on a test or
quiz and we always encouraged each other to
study harder.

This remarkable teacher is also well-loved as a coach. To her
volleyball team she is "Mama" and she is considered "a drill
sergeant" on the court and "a good friend" on the sidelines by
former students who remember brutal morning practices and a
coach who instilled in them a "passion for athletics" never to
be forgotten.

Leanne Iravanni motivates in many ways using "great praise
and the odd dozen doughnuts" according to one student. But,
above all, she stirs the crowd in a way best explained by her principal, who says that there is not a day that the lives of students
and staff are not touched by the presence of this interesting
woman. She brings exciting issues to both the classroom and
staffroom and adds fun to everyone's learning life at school.
Daily, colleagues learn a little biology when they open the
staffroom refrigerator and face her latest specimen from the local
abattoir. And while the specimens are dead, her classes are alive
with enthusiasm, lively pace and grounded theory.

Never the aloof scientist, this exciting teacher participates in
all aspects of the school fabric. In addition to coaching volleyball, she runs the student council, acts as adviser to the outdoor
education club and supervises exchange trips, doing all with spirit
and panache.

Grenville Bray

Gren Bray is a firecracker. This tall, lank, rather sober-looking
man explodes in teaching with more energy than a school full
of young students. He bounds into rooms with a long, bounc-
ing gait, eyes flashing, smile alight, radiating an enthusiasm that
could only be measured in megawatts.

Gren was born and raised in a small city in the heart of tourist
country, an area that is snowbound and lonely in winter and
overrun with cottagers in summer. He has continued to live there

and has taught most of his professional career, over twenty years, in the same region.

He is a hometown boy made good, a homebody, well grounded in community, committed to traditional values and lifestyle.

And yet Gren travels on a regular basis. In summer, his vacation is spent as a volunteer with medical missionaries in South America, bringing gifts of sight through eyeglasses collected with commitment over the winter.

He also takes flight in spring and fall when baseball beckons and he begins to follow his beloved Blue Jays, taking in as many home and away games as possible, usually as the loudest cheerleader in the stands.

At home, his enthusiasm is applied to his community and his elementary school with equal zeal. He teaches; he coaches; he directs; he organizes. When the yearly town fair is opened with a parade, everyone's favorite teacher, Gren Bray, often leads the way as parade marshall.

His students, past and present, talk about his talent as an athlete and musician, his energy, his willingness to give up his free time, the fun he brings to the classroom. Whether it be basketball, volleyball, choir or drama, each new experience with this dynamic teacher is as interesting and exciting as the last.

Through his personal energy, Gren is able to take the school to the community. With zeal his students fill the local park in the fall for borderball games and entertain people with musicals such as *The Wizard of Oz*. They also have informed the home town of issues such as famine in a dramatic way when Gren organized a group of students in a thirty-hour fast for World Vision.

His current principal, another of his fans, says about Gren Bray:

> From the very first day in the school, he made
> a distinct impression upon me. Although he
> has been teaching for close to twenty years,
> he possesses the energy and enthusiasm of a
> first-year teacher. He brings a strong love of
> his world and the people in it to the school
> every day.

Marie-Claire Bourgeois

For Marie-Claire Bourgeois, becoming a primary school teacher was like coming home. She grew up in Schefferville, in Northern Quebec, surrounded by young children since her mother ran a day care centre. After high school, she left home for university and she is now, once again, surrounded by young children — this time because she is teaching Grade 1 French immersion in Ontario.

Marie-Claire Bourgeois was nominated Teacher of the Year by almost every parent of her students who forwarded an unbeatable package of letters. Their comments indicated that this impressive teacher produces weekly reports on each child, rewards achievement with tokens that are redeemable at the classroom store, organizes special "theme" lunches, individualizes both program and approach to suit each child and in general "transforms the lives of her young students."

Carolyn Grant, a parent who nominated her, wrote:

> Academically, "Madame" Bourgeois provides
> the children with lots of learning opportunities
> while preparing them for the challenges which
> will come in subsequent school years.

In size Marie-Claire is almost as small as the first-graders she teaches; in impact, she towers above the ordinary.

Never content to accept the standard, she inspires her young students with every motivational approach possible. She sews with them, she prepares special meals, she takes them out in the community and above all she teaches, teaches, teaches.

As one parent stated:

> Not any one method of teaching works for all
> students. Madame Bourgeois is aware of this
> and is able to combine the best of each
> method of teaching, whether that be a combi-
> nation of whole language and phonics, or the
> combination of child-centred learning, one-on-
> one teaching and teaching to the whole class.
> "Madame" uses all types of teaching to
> ensure that the children are exposed to
> different ways of learning.

Her energetic and varied approach to learning holds interest for all students, and as a result, parents constantly remark on the improvement in attitude that they find in their children. The students in her class go the extra mile, from speaking French in the schoolyard to sorting their Hallowe'en treats into categories and producing bar graphs of them.

As with most interesting people, Marie-Claire Bourgeois takes chances.

> She is not intimidated. Neither the board, her principal nor any parent can sway her vision and attitude. She is strong-minded and determined to provide the learning experience on her terms. What that ultimately means is that the child is the winner.
>
> Over the past two decades, teachers have taken a rollercoaster ride in the attempt to satisfy their superiors and parents. This political distraction has led to a decrease in the effectiveness of the vast majority of those in the teaching profession.
>
> Not so with Marie-Claire Bourgeois. Her single-mindedness and attention to what is best and most interesting for the children, has led to a superior life-learning environment.
>
> My daughter wants to go to school each day. She admires, respects and pays attention to what her teacher says. She knows that Marie-Claire cares for her as a person and wants her to do her best at all times. She knows her teacher is tough. She knows her teacher is very demanding. She knows her teacher gives her an incredible amount of work, including homework. She loves it. She has learned so much in so little time. She has confidence and enthusiasm.

William J. Oliver

In looks, in experience, in actions, Bill Oliver is an educational hot shot, a towering red-headed leader who has never lost his team spirit or his drive and forward focus.

Bill Oliver began teaching in Scarborough in 1963. With whirlwind speed he moved from classroom to administration and there he has made his mark ever since, not just by serving as the head of a school but by infiltrating the hearts and souls of the student body.

This principal *extraordinaire* is, indeed, a model of excellence. He sets the pace for others by continually coaching sports teams, by remaining involved in front-line teaching, by community and professional leadership in the fight for safe schools and by bringing fun back into the professional profile through his magic acts and his skills as a juggler.

Bill Oliver was not put forth for this award by an obvious nominator — that is, someone in direct contact with him through athletic teams or his outreach work. No, Sasha Singh, the student who nominated this topnotch principal, comes from the general student body. She wrote:

> Mr. Oliver supports every activity the school has to offer. He is everywhere. He listens to us. He has such a close relationship with many students that he will even spend time after school shooting hoops. One might think that I am on one of his sports teams, in an academic club or in the drama company, but I'm not. I am just a regular student who has never had any direct contact with Mr. Oliver, but has still felt his influence greatly. I do believe that I speak for everyone when I say he is our teacher of the year.

Here is a man with inexhaustible energy who seems to be interested in every aspect of a student's life in his school. He does it all with an elan and humor that stagger his colleagues. He has filled a mind-boggling series of positions of leadership in his professional organization of secondary school teachers.

Even his hobby is filled with fun ... and opportunities for teaching. He could earn his living as a juggler and magician.

Not a student can be unimpressed by the excitement that surrounds this extraordinary human being. And a teacher-principal

40

who is so interesting provides a role model for both students and colleagues. All of them are thrilled to know that he thinks what they are doing is so important that he cannot take his mind off them for a moment.

> He truly wants to see us get the most out of high school — no matter what our interests may be. He always find the time to praise each of the teams and clubs for the excellent work they've done — win or lose. He is more than happy to talk to any student about any problem he/she might have. I guess one could say he is quite approachable. To give an idea of how close he is to his students, he never condemns any of us for making fun of his red hair and his height (he is very tall). At many performances, he is the ''butt-end'' of our jokes, but he knows it is all in good fun. Mr. Oliver is often in the hallways having humorous conversations with the students and never hesitates to say hello when one passes by.
> Mr. Oliver also takes the time to answer the many concerns of our community. He also has close contact with our parents and meets with them frequently to discuss our developments in school. He promotes integration and lets his views be known by making television appearances to discuss his concerns about high school students.

SUMMARY

Students are a captive audience. All children must go to school, at least until a certain age. Long after most required military service has been abandoned, schooling remains compulsory around the world. In fact, sitting in class remains one of the few experiences in our lives in which we are compelled by the state to listen and respond to a person.

No wonder so many students simply go to school but refuse

to take their daily dose. They attend, but little more. Our schools are haunted by these students who end up under-achieving. They are the students who chronically complain of boredom.

In this regard, it can be said that while there may be compulsory attendance in our schools, there isn't compulsory education.

To learn requires interest. To spark this interest in students, a teacher must have the confidence of teachers like "Mr. P.," "Mama," the "Cookie Monster," "Madame," and "Coach," namely the confidence to go beyond the lesson plan.

These teachers would be dynamos in any job. In most positions, they would receive extra status and considerable remuneration. Perhaps only in the unique world of teaching does such performance receive little immediate reinforcement. But it is also the case that successful teaching provides enormous satisfaction when the result is that young people are better because of one's own work. Surely this is more important than status and money. It has to be!

CHAPTER 4

The Available Teacher

The term "available" does not stir the blood or arouse the excitement that more passionate descriptions of teachers might elicit. However, being a teacher has more to do with relationships than with contact hours.

Unfortunately, students do not see the full spectrum of a teacher's life. They are unaware that teachers have their own families to look after, other interests to pursue, volunteer activities to accommodate, financial pressures and all sorts of other stresses outside the classroom.

People, particularly adolescents, can be very self-centred and impatient. If they think they're being ignored or overlooked, they begin to believe the myth that a teacher who is not omnipresent and focussed on every individual student just does not care about them. The wise teacher is open and frank about her personal timetable and thereby reduces the tension inherent between the expectations of students and parents on the one hand, and the rights of teachers to a private life on the other.

Nonetheless, the fact remains that unless students have access to teachers when they really need them, the process of learning is eroded.

Cliff Nuttall

Cliff Nuttall is a giant of a man who has played football in the Rose Bowl, surely one of the most prestigious of all athletic events in the United States, and has represented Canada at the Olympics as a record-breaking track and field athlete.

He is now a physical education teacher and he has achieved an extraordinary level of interaction with the students in his suburban high school. As one of them described:

> I feel that a great amount of learning goes on outside the class as well as in the class setting. Mr. Nuttall is a prime example in both areas as he has arranged many activities for his students to take part in. Those activities include after-school sports, a canoe trip every spring and fall for the past twenty years, and on many occasions [he] has taken personal time to assist students who have obtained very high levels in track and field. These examples are only a few.
>
> Mr. Nuttall has also shown us that practice, determination and dedication will pay off. Although Mr. Nuttall has achieved many awards in his life, all his focus now is on bettering the skills and attitudes of students. Almost every night, after school, he and many other students including myself, attend the weight room in our school. Mr. Nuttall assists students with weight training and flexibility training. This is one of the reasons, that, in my mind, puts him beyond many other physical education teachers. He teaches by example. Even after a long life of high school, college, and teaching for 25 years he still stays in shape.

Cliff Nuttall is a local fellow. Although he went on to international glory, he has returned to teach in the community that he grew up in near the farm his family first settled over a century ago.

As a student, Cliff credits one particular teacher who was available to him as a mentor and role model for all his later successes. Now he himself has become a mentor and a role model. Much like the beloved teacher whom he feels had a far-reaching influence on him, he is available to his students.

"Never settle for second-best" is his most frequent admonition, and it is in relation to schoolwork as well as basketball or track and field.

A colleague, the school's guidance counsellor, wrote about Cliff Nuttall:

> At the administrative level, and as a teacher, Cliff has touched the lives of thousands of young people both directly and indirectly. He has developed and delivered programs which have enriched students' lives during their school years, and long after graduation. This year, on two separate occasions, parents have said that Cliff was directly responsible for their teens' decision to remain in school.

More than merely putting in long hours, this imposing 6'5" former Olympic athlete serves his students relentlessly. Extra time is never denied. More importantly he can always be found to give the extra help to the unhelpable and support and attention to the vulnerable. He is big, strong, smart and accomplished. But more than anything he does for his students, he is theirs.

Perhaps the most moving statement in support of Cliff Nuttall's teaching excellence came from his principal, who wrote:

> As Cliff's principal for ten years I realized that he is not merely an excellent teacher, coach and friend to his students but also has a heart that reaches out to the child who is the loner, the trouble-maker, the child others wish to avoid. Cliff has probably changed hundreds of young people's lives by simply being himself.

To dismiss Cliff Nuttall as an example of an extraordinary world-class athlete whose natural ability and youthful exploits have accorded him a career in teaching based on the glories of the past would be glib and wrong. Only performance in the present can influence young people with short memories.

Nuttall knows that only his day-by-day commitment to the learning of his students gives them the reason to emulate the quality of his life and work.

Brenda McKelvie

Brenda McKelvie is an educated educator. She has several degrees which include a master's degree and a doctorate in education, and she has researched and published studies on our university system.

In teaching terms, Brenda has yet to settle down. Thus far she has worked as a supply teacher, accepting only temporary contracts.

A supply teacher rarely receives any attention, let alone adulation. The assumption is that such an individual has but a part-time commitment to the profession and forms few, if any, important relationships with students or colleagues.

It was a shock indeed to discover that Brenda, a teacher wishing to spend only certain months in the classroom, had been nominated as a Teacher of the Year. The nomination, of course, was based not on her availability over a year but rather on her overtime availability during any work day.

Our memories of replacements for regular staff members are often laced with amusement and guilt. Stories of having confused and frustrated such poor souls are legion. Students took on new identities, provided bizarre and totally erroneous information about lessons covered or subject material omitted and generally took advantage of the situation to misbehave.

Yet here is an occasional teacher who is described by an administrator as follows:

> She's fabulous. She's one of the most professional people I have ever met. Immense knowledge. Incredibly creative. She has graduate degrees yet she continuously takes courses. She is into cooperative group learning and has high expectations of kids. She is caring and cooperative and works unbelievable hours. She works well as a team partner and is great at modifying programs to meet needs of kids.

As well as substitute teaching, Brenda McKelvie has been available after the traditional timetable for a student at the school who had cancer and needed to be taught at home. They met in the classroom and this supply teacher was the child's first choice as tutor when treatment made school attendance impossible.

In her winning letter of nomination the student, then in Grade 7, wrote:

> Hi! I'm Lena Daley. I'm a grade 7 student and I'd like to nominate my tutor, Brenda McKelvie, as the Toronto Sun Teacher of the Year. She is also a substitute teacher for a grade 3 class at my school. She was assigned to be my tutor last year in March after I was diagnosed with neuroblastoma (cancer). After putting in a full day's work at school, around 3 times a week or more she either comes to my home or to McMaster Children's Hospital in Hamilton.
>
> I'm nominating Mrs. McKelvie not just because of the school work but also for the laughter, the support and even the odd lecture when I needed it. She knows when my blood count's low or after chemotherapy that I've got very little energy. She therefore schedules my work so that I do the hardest stuff when I'm feeling better. I hope she wins because she cares and I couldn't have done it all without her!

Obviously, Brenda McKelvie does not know how to teach with a part-time commitment. And though she has yet to "sign on the dotted line" with a full-time contract, she is a perfect model of continuous education.

One of the disconcerting aspects of the teaching profession is its lack of attention to the preparation of new teachers. The faculties of education have but a year to train them, to dispense the bare essentials and assist in providing survival techniques for the initial year of teaching. Although good teachers are normally involved with education faculties during weeks of practice teaching, no one believes that this one year represents adequate preparation. Brenda McKelvie is a reminder of what could be accomplished if teachers were organized to provide mentoring for teachers through the first years of their professional lives.

In fact, even as a supply teacher, she has made herself available to student teachers, a role which is not normally expected from occasional staff members. One student teacher described his observations of this job-enriching teacher:

> Mrs. McKelvie continually identifies and works on the different needs of each student. She is interested in their activities outside the school, which I feel is significant to a teacher/student rapport. It is an honor to be exposed to an exceptional role model. She exemplifies the many qualities discussed at the faculty of a "good teacher."

The good teacher is a confident teacher. Brenda McKelvie hands out a report card form which every child is invited to fill in. The subject of the card's evaluation is her own teaching. A courageous indication that all are learners and all need evaluation — and proof of her availability and sense of accountability.

As we enter an age when part-time work may be the norm rather than the exception, Brenda McKelvie may be pointing the way to a satisfying professional lifestyle. Her commitment of time may be occasional but the commitment of her spirit is total.

Lena Daley died just twenty-four months after she wrote the winning nomination of Brenda McKelvie as Teacher of the Year. The teacher and student remained a team until the end and, indeed, were together for Lena's last hour. Honors aside, they were there for each other, between the accolades, beyond the expected, beside the pain.

Lena made sure that the world would understand what made her teacher special; she spearheaded her public tribute as Teacher of the Year.

In return, Brenda McKelvie will ensure that no one forgets her favorite student, the child to whom she has had a memorial plaque inscribed and hung in her school, the child who taught her about life and about death and whose memory will never let her forget the impact a teacher can have on the lives around her.

Connie Sanders

Our picture of the teacher normally features an adult, usually female, surrounded by smiling children. Rarely do we acknowledge that learning is becoming a lifetime commitment on the part of every person, young or old.

To be a parent, a citizen or an employee demands complex preparation. The role of the teacher has been changed forever by the fact that continuing education is now commonplace. No longer is the elementary teacher simply preparing students for a secondary school experience, nor is the secondary teacher preoccupied only with the provision of training to cope with a job or post-secondary education. Both are intervenors in the life-long education of every student they meet.

There are now many teachers who work only with adults. One of them is Connie Sanders. She teaches law, world and Canadian history and social studies at an open-door adult learning centre to people who dropped out of school but now, as adults, realize how important it is to re-engage in studies which will make them more employable. Teaching in such a program involves the ultimate form of accountability — the immediate satisfaction of learning goals as defined by mature individuals quite able to discern their own needs.

Connie recognizes that most of her students have been defeated by the formal educational system. She regards her job as being about lighting a fire of enthusiasm for learning that will make it easier for them to find employment. But it is also much more than that. These people will likely move through many jobs over the course of their careers. How can a few months of time in a classroom arouse an intellectual curiosity, a desire to learn, and provide an introduction to knowledge that will serve as a source of personal confidence, job after job, throughout a lifetime of employment? How can a teacher express in a few symbolic actions, a hint of those elements of caring and compassion that will assist people to live lives not of quiet desperation but of satisfaction? The words of an enthusiastic student give a glimpse of the depth of concern that Connie exhibits for these grown-up students.

This well-travelled lady makes learning a joy.
She imparts her knowledge in such a way that

she practically paints word pictures in her students' minds.

Connie gives of herself to her classes. For example, she makes birthday cakes for her students on their special day; provides supplies and instructs students on making chocolate candles at Christmas and Valentine day... all at her own expense. These are extra-curricular activities so she is also giving of her free time. She takes numerous snapshots of her students while they are engaged in various programs and provides a "Wall of Fame," as it were, in her classroom giving the students a feeling of belonging. There is no negativism in this lady's make-up. She is a booster and it shows in the attitudes of her students toward learning. She gives them an import of self-worth. Teaching adults is not an easy job but Connie seems to welcome each student, not as a challenge but as a new success story about to unfold. I was one of these success stories. I returned to school after an absence of 42 years, having received my earlier education in another country. I graduated with honors.

Availability to her students includes a strategy of involving politicians, lawyers, judges and policemen as representatives of the outside world. Connie brings that world into her classroom but also takes her students out into the community, visiting courtrooms, municipal council chambers and any other place in which her pupils can learn.

For Connie Sanders, learning is a societal affair and takes place in a panoply of venues restricted only by a narrow vision of both learner and teacher. The intimacy of shared learning is expressed in her own words as quoted in her local newspaper:

We become very close. We share their tragedies, they share ours. We all have something to learn. Me, I just have a diploma and a degree. They have more of an education of life than I have.

A good teacher, not only of adults but of students of all ages, is able to draw out the knowledge and experience of people and give it pattern, direction and meaning. Teachers of quality respect and value what students have already acquired, remembered or sought out. Every such teacher becomes a fellow learner in the journey of lifelong education. This is a form of emotional and intellectual availability that is priceless.

Gerry Gibson

Gerry Gibson is not just a teacher who is there when students have learning and personal needs to discuss with someone they can trust. He is an individual who reaches out to children before their difficulties undermine their confidence and self-respect. Such is the essence of the available teacher.

In the workplace, Gerry Gibson flies in the face of tradition. He teaches elementary school. As our society attempts to deal with the continuing and changing challenges of establishing more positive gender roles, we are coming to realize how defeating it is to have female teachers dominating the classrooms of our elementary schools and male colleagues concentrated in the secondary and post-secondary — particularly graduate school — levels of our educational system. The implicit message of such segregation is not lost on students: real men do not nurture; caring for the young is women's work. In effect, this stereotype suggests that elementary school is the glorified playpen of our learning system, and that the "important" education takes place after children have entered high school or university. Yet everything we have learned about education indicates that the early years are crucial for laying the foundation for success in learning for the rest of a lifetime. Gerry Gibson, as a model, speaks to this significance.

No wonder he was nominated by his entire school community, by students, by colleagues and by parents. At the time he was teaching a triple-graded primary class, surely an exercise in individual attention. Not only did he face this challenge, but his school was in its first year of operation after a closure for declining enrolment that had lasted five years. An inspired decision by an administrator sent Gerry to the newly reopened school, not only as a teacher of early elementary grades, but as a leader who could provide advice and be a model for other teachers facing the problems of resuscitating an institution.

Accolades abound in the documents supporting his nomination:

> That Gerry is kind, considerate, intelligent, articulate, organized, committed to a child- and experience-centred program, knowledge- able about the latest computer technology and a practitioner of the most effective teaching methodologies is not what sets him apart from the rest of us. I believe what really sets Gerry apart, what makes him the inspiring and respected leader he is, is his unique ability to share.

The most important sharing takes place in relation to a profound understanding both of how children learn, and of what they must learn if they are to cope with the complex, inter-related, interdisciplinary problems confronting our planet.

> He has conducted an entire program around the theme of birds. He used learning about birds as the backdrop for learning about units of measurement (building a birdhouse), reading (spelling lists of your favorite birds), geography (how different climates have different species), and so on. He invited in special guests and generally provided my child's class with a love of nature in one of its most beautiful manifestations.

Gerry teaches in a large city with an unparalleled variety of children with ethnic, religious, language and dress differences. Multiculturalism has become both the pride and the problem of the urban school. But Gibson sees only the opportunity which presents itself to the sensitive teacher.

> He has recently undertaken a large role in the Caribbean Week of the school. His class is preparing a couple of genuine Caribbean

songs for presentation at an assembly; they will also learn of the geography and, of course, the contribution in terms of immigration that these wonderful islands have made to our Canadian culture.

Mr Gibson found himself this year with a grade 3 student who spoke no English in September. Both her parents were new Canadians and had little grasp of the language. He has worked very hard at integrating the child into the classroom in a way that is comfortable for all. More than that, he has, on several occasions, gone out of his way to translate things like birthday invitations for the little girl and her mother so she can be included in these celebrations which are so important to children's self-esteem at this age. He has done this with kindness and tact.

Gerry knows that sharing, a form of availability, can be learned. One of the most important lessons for today is that a voluntary contribution to any community program may be a source of satisfaction that rivals the love of vocation that has dominated our century.

SUMMARY

Students equate contact with teachers outside the classroom setting with true caring. In the minds of young people, the time a teacher puts in in class represents "the job of being a teacher." It has as much to do with being a custodian as it does with being an instructor. The teacher whose commitment extends beyond the legal niceties of the nine-to-four period is seen as a friend, a confidante, indeed a partner in learning.

A true professional is often described as a worker who does not "punch a time clock" and although it is common knowledge that teachers spend countless hours at their desks both at school and at home, this behavior is invisible and easily forgotten.

Knowing that a teacher is available, both physically and intellectually, means a lot to students because it shows that the teacher is interested in the whole person and goes beyond the expected process of recognizing capacity and identifying weakness. It involves a generosity of spirit that enriches every learning life.

CHAPTER 5

The Informed Teacher

One cannot teach unless one has something to teach. No matter what the subject, a good teacher must be informed, indeed must exhibit a mastery of his or her discipline if the magic of learning is to transpire. Effective teaching technique is essential, but it is nothing without knowledge in the subject a teacher intends to convey to students.

The teacher best remembered is someone who has such an enthusiasm and delight in the subject, that the excitement bubbles over in every class. This dedication to knowledge may result in behavior that seems obsessive — constant reading and subsequent discussion of the latest books or articles — but it's a process that enhances the active and curious mind. Or it may inspire attendance at lectures, workshops, concerts and plays that explore the latest developments in the field. Or it may enable a teacher to use televison as a window of true learning. Whatever the medium, a "turned-on" teacher uses it to pass information on to students who then share the excitement and come to see learning as both a personal pursuit and a collective responsibility.

The point to be made is that each of us has encountered a teacher whose commitment to continuous learning has been evident and whose expertise has been a source of awe, respect and interest.

It is such encounters that have driven countless young people to become teachers themselves or attracted them to make vocational choices involving the subject matter these splendid teachers have taught them. Teaching is an art that, like wine, improves with age. The faculty of education or teacher's college may provide survival skills for that first year in front of a class, but it can do little more. It is in the crucible of day-to-day teaching reinforced by up-to-date knowledge and expertise that the superb teacher emerges.

Richard Van Duzer

Richard Van Duzer has become a living legend after thirty years in a high school in a small city. He is known affectionately in his school as "The Chief" or "The Professor." Richard is coming to the end of his long career as a teacher of history and politics. It is apparent that his energy and enthusiasm are undiminished and the response of his students is as appreciative as it ever was.

It is the strong base of information and understanding in his discipline that empowers Richard to create a unique atmosphere in his class. He uses humor to great effect, relieving the tension inherent in any institutionalized experience, and his humor comes from a natural comfort he has with his subject. His stature as a scholar is so firm that he can correct students gently and informally without arousing resentment and threatening the kinds of humiliations that can be so destructive in the learning environment. He can expand his tools of the trade to visuals that point up the drama of historic occasions — his collection of vintage election posters and lapel buttons is but one measure of his imaginative rendering of the past in the present.

The popular designation "Professor" recognizes his intellectual attainment as defined by his students. One expressed his appreciation by writing that Richard "can provide a story on any topic at the snap of a finger." His further comment that he "relates history to his own life stories" reveals that here is a teacher who fits his own experience into the "story" and encourages students to see themselves as part of that story. This surely is an essential road to interest and relevance in a history class.

How can one assess the long-term effect of such a teacher? On the basis of the man whose family is convinced that Van Duzer's influence was the crucial element that led to a Ph.D. from Oxford? Or does one give even more attention to the dozens of letters from graduates who are now appreciating in later life how important those lessons in "The Professor's" class really were?

How does a teacher reach this height of respect? By the most obvious strategy imaginable. The great teacher is a great learner. The teacher who is trading on an undergraduate degree — or even a post-graduate degree of some years past — can never attain the awe of students. Teaching involves a constant struggle to find time to read, to research and, in some cases, to write. A good teacher must regard it as a part of his or her task to be as up-to-date as the latest periodical report or newspaper reference. An impossible expectation? Undoubtedly. And the greatest frustration for many teachers is that of straining towards this goal. It is the price one must pay if one is to arouse and excite students who may have access to more information than their predecessors.

Everyone at Richard Van Duzer's school, and indeed in his town, knows him as "The Professor" because he is accepted as a local fountain of knowledge and specific information. He teaches with this solid foundation and thus respect is his — never demanded, always gained.

But this is not a detached intellectual. His cache of wisdom includes his vast collection of memorabilia, palpable traces of the past.

No wonder this historian and political specialist can make the past explain the present so effectively, so thoroughly and so knowledgeably.

Joan Phillips

There are few teaching jobs more difficult than that of Joan Phillips and the team she leads in the preschool program at Erinoak Treatment Centre. There are few children more demanding to care for, more complex to program for, few children with futures more precarious than those of the children who enter the centre with many medical problems described by reams of reports. Their prognosis for walking and talking is rarely certain. Some neither see nor hear. Most often their developmental profiles bear the dreaded diagnosis, "It is doubtful that..." Nonetheless, upon admission, regardless of medical or psychological pessimism, Joan Phillips and the staff she supervises set to work to improve each child's odds and to remove the doubts about development.

Not only do these educators teach special students, they are, both by action and by definition, very special themselves. Their mandate is to bring education to those children for whom many doors to learning are shut. In many cases, they teach the unteachable.

To plan an individualized program for such learners demands more than optimism. The successful education of each exceptional student depends on the highly specialized knowledge of each exceptional educator.

To begin, Joan Phillips must be able to collect and integrate information from a range of professionals in many diverse disciplines such as general and neonatal medicine, neurology, orthopaedics, ophthalmology, psychology, genetics, nursing and social work. She must then attempt to understand each child within the context of the pain and confusion that invariably mark the lives of children whose early development is abnormal.

In this respect, Joan Phillips acts as an interpreter, taking masses of information from others, then adding direct observation supplemented by her own immense knowledge of child development and translating it all into a beneficial program plan.

Moreover, she is always on the alert, ever-ready to change her approach, to redesign, to revamp.

And even though each child in her care presents a unique learning challenge, Joan Phillips remains goal-directed. Tomorrow will be somewhat better than today.

Hope is always alive and well in her program.

Joan Phillips was nominated Teacher of the Year by a parent, in memory of her daughter. Angela Manasterski died suddenly just before her fourth birthday. After her death, her mother put forth the name of her favorite teacher for honors because she knew that Joan Phillips and the staff at the centre had helped give Angela the best life she could have had.

Despite the sad outcome, this supporter's words were full of optimism.

About her child's education she said:

> With Joan Phillips at Erinoak Angela
> responded so much and accomplished so
> much despite how little the doctors had
> thought possible.
>   I came into the classroom one day not too

long before she died and saw Angela sitting
by herself, this was truly a wonderful thing
to happen especially when she could only sit
with support before, and this time she was
balancing herself with her hands. Then when
I walked up to her she looked up at me,
which is something else she could never do
before. You have no idea how that made me
feel. I will always remember her smile.

Intricate knowledge of the complex development of exceptional
children should go along with a balance of tender compassion
with tough love. A teacher like Joan Phillips must make demands
of students and drive them to achieve beyond their families'
dreams. To be informed about every complicated detail of every
complicated child's potential is an educational struggle that
demands constant learning and monitoring.

Gloria Howard

Through her wealth of experience in education, Gloria Howard
has become very informed about students, educational programs
and schools. Over the past thirty years, she has taught a range
of subjects which include history, world religion and special education. Few teachers ever face such a variety of challenges in subject matter and diversity of students or have the opportunity to
gain so much information about the field while on the job. She
is equally knowledgeable about front-line teaching and administration and has been able to reach the full continuum of students
from the gifted to the disadvantaged learner, from teenager to
adult. She has been a vice-principal at a night school for many
years, and she was a founder of a school for the performing arts.

In a field that prides itself on being all things to all people,
Gloria Howard is, indeed, a well-rounded example.

As with most of the models of excellence in this book, Gloria
Howard could serve to illustrate any of our six standards of success. It is, however, her knowledge of the system, her information base for students that led to her recognition as a Teacher
of the Year.

She was nominated by a former student who first met Ms.

Howard in her Grade 11 world religion class. The student, like many, was turned off by school and only waiting to turn sixteen and leave formal education far behind. Besides hating school, she was going though a time of personal upheaval. Her parents had just separated. She began to skip classes and most of her year was spent in the principal's office. She remembers that her only comfortable times in school after the primary grades were in Gloria Howard's world religion class and she describes her as the first teacher who cared about her learning, and who wanted to help her understand the importance of her total education, not just one specific class.

However, this contact with a favorite teacher was not enough for the teenager, and ultimately truancy and general underachievement caught up with her. She was asked to leave the school.

She did, fortunately, return the next year. This time the hookup was cemented and teacher and student evolved into a successful team. In fact, Gloria Howard's nomination was written by the student upon whom she made an impact far beyond specific content, long after every one else had her branded as ''bad,'' and long before her potential was obvious.

Ironically, the nomination was written longhand on several pages of teacher's planning paper.

The former drop-out has become a colleague. She is now a teacher herself and she credits her mentor for pointing the way:

> I remember looking at a schedule to see what
> she was teaching. It said Economics. Without
> knowing what economics was, I signed up for
> the course only because she was teaching.

In this way learning begot learning and teaching begot teaching. Gloria Howard provided information about a subject and, in the process, the subject became learning and the golden goal of education was reached.

> I went on to university and completed a
> degree in philosophy. I then applied to
> teachers' college. It had been a dream of mine
> to be able to touch and make a positive differ-
> ence in children's lives, the way Mrs. Howard
> did mine.

I am now in my second year of teaching. My experiences with Mrs. Howard have helped me to understand that teaching is much more than academics. If I can become half the teacher Mrs. Howard is, I will feel that my job as an educator has reached a standard I can be proud of.

In my graduation yearbook she wrote..."At times you may feel 'anger' with me — at times, you may even 'love' me. But all in total, we have had a couple of good years together. I know that we shall not be strangers in the future." She was right.

Mrs. Howard continued to be there for me. When I applied to the school board, I am convinced that her letter of reference secured my interview.

As you can see she is quite a person. I am very proud to have been one of Mrs. Howard's students and I feel privileged to now be one of Gloria's colleagues.

To be honest, I can't believe she has not won this award every year.

Gloria Howard's career begs the question, "What is basic justice in a classroom of thirty or so students?" There are some who would argue that each student deserves the same quota of attention. Others would suggest that the outstanding teacher recognizes that certain students need different access at certain points in their learning life than others. The teacher who, like Gloria Howard, has extensive knowledge of both her subject and her students, can sense the needs, the desperation, the frustration, the despair of particular students, and intervene appropriately, is a model of the informed teacher to be emulated and honored as a Teacher of the Year.

Jean Eliopoulos Sena

Jean Sena says she has always been single-minded in her career goals; ever since she played house she pretended to be a teacher.

When she was ten years old she came to Canada from Greece and after high school, diplomas and degrees in education followed as an automatic part of her lifeplan.

Jean has taught for the same school board ever since her student teacher placement there ten years ago. She quite simply loves her job and says that the students and their parents have taught her everything she knows.

Obviously, her students and their parents are equally enthusiastic about this teacher. When asked to name a Teacher of the Year, MacKenzie Sutherland and family did not submit one nomination for Jean Sena; they wrote a letter a day, every day from January to March.

Here is an example of one parent's comments about the winning teacher:

> Mrs. Sena's classes are like MAGIC — there is
> no other word to describe just how she
> teaches. I often refer to her as "Sidney
> Poitier" of To Sir with Love or as "Robin
> Williams" in Dead Poets Society.
>   No one deserves this award more than Mrs.
> Sena. You would never forget in a million
> years how this great teacher touched the lives
> of so many people. I only wish that I had had
> a teacher that made such a difference — that
> challenged each individual to be their best —
> to reach their goals and strive for perfection.

The magic that Jean Sena weaves is based on ongoing research about each of her charges. To be able to challenge a student continually demands a continuous flow of information about that child. Her director of education describes her as thus informed when he states:

> An inquiring mind and an outstanding sense
> of purpose are the key attributes of this fine
> educator. Jean makes people feel valued for
> their ideas and for their contribution.

She listens; she asks; she takes time to know all her students a little better. She gathers information about her students, not unlike a squirrel preparing for winter, never wasting the chance to listen, to understand, to store facts for later use.

I would frequently observe her at the school entry seeking out a parent for a brief talk.

An informed teacher must not stop short with only scholarly supports. To understand young children also demands personal information that does not rest in books or files and professional problem-solving that can be shared. In this regard, Jean is an informed teacher *par excellence*, able to learn, able to share, able to grow as she helps her students and colleagues to do the same.

Inside the classroom, what immediately struck me about Jean was her ability to share ownership of the class with others. The librarian, guidance teacher and myself were regularly included in the classroom program as it is Jean's belief that children benefit greatly from a wide range of interactions with adults. Jean encouraged me in my interest in teaching language through music and provided many occasions for me to be actively involved in her class. On monthly calendars home to the parents, Jean would be certain to include all teachers' names who had interacted with her class.

Jean also believes that children can teach each other, and daily encourages them to be considerate and caring. I have commented to Jean that there seems to be a kind of magic about the learning atmosphere in her room — children quietly and happily working together, in a spirit of friendship and trust.

A quiet and reflective person, Jean is always focussed on the needs of the students, parents and staff.

Paul Brisley

Paul Brisley is an elementary teacher *extraordinaire* with the unbeatable combination of brain and brawn. He is an athlete who teaches music, a dramatic artist who plays ball.

Growing up in Toronto he began teaching there and then moved to northern Ontario and taught for two years in Moosonee. After the next eight years back in the city, he moved in 1980 to his current placement in a middle school, in a small town with rural roots.

Paul is impressive as a teacher because he is always visible as a working, well-informed model. He not only teaches music, he performs professionally, he stages local musical productions, he directs concerts. He not only coaches teams, he plays baseball and football.

As a result, students know that the information he provides has meaning and application. They see results. They gain direction. What better proof of the usefulness of school information than a teacher who practises what he preaches, especially when that teacher loves both the content material he is imparting and the process of imparting it?

One of his fellow teachers wrote:

> As a colleague I admire this man as a knowledgeable teacher par excellence, and respect the exemplary professional standards that he consistently models. During an in-service session this year, a few among us voiced concerns around increased responsibilities, stress and the ever-changing programs teachers are expected to deliver. Mr. Brisley, ending the meeting on a positive note, stated: "We have the best jobs in the world. On a daily basis we have an opportunity to make a difference in the lives of kids."
>
> While morale in education may be very low at the present time, exellence in this classroom is the norm. Beyond Music skills, Mr. Brisley has indeed taught children about discipline, commitment and self-respect. As a colleague, I so much respect the energy, time and dedication he has for his work. As you watch him teach, you just know he loves every minute of it.

SUMMARY

One of the greatest frustrations for teachers is the knowledge that they daily fall behind in the arduous task of being on top of their chosen field or fields of expertise. The information revolution, with its explosion of new data, its ever-increasing flow of articles and books, leaves teachers whose time is taken up with lesson preparation, classroom performance and student evaluation in a constant state of shock.

As the models of excellence in this chapter demonstrate, informed teachers must be much more than a mere bookworm to be successful. Academic wisdom, knowledge of child development, learning and systems theory, and individual differences are the sources of information from which they create professional success.

Being master or mistress of a skill or a body of knowledge, and understanding the needs of each student are laudable signs of an informed teacher. In particular, colleagues, especially those who are less experienced, look to such persons as models.

In the very difficult days that lie ahead, the teachers who read widely and well and integrate this knowledge into the very lessons preparing young people to face the world will be treasures in whatever community they serve. The next century may well be about the transformation of our values and behaviors and blessed indeed will be the student who is touched by the insight and wisdom of such a teacher.

CHAPTER 6

The Accountable Teacher

In decades past, accountability was defined as little more than presence, that is, being on site in the classroom for the hours required by the Education Act. And, of course, it was also deemed important that order be kept if property was to be protected and the physical well-being of students was to be assured.

In more recent years, the emphasis on accountability has shifted dramatically to outcomes, and the learning function in the classroom has become tied to academic results, usually connected to "objective" tests and compared to the perceived success of students in other lands. Often it was not clear whether the varying results of these tests reflected different curricula or at least subject emphasis, whether the students were comparable from jurisdiction to jurisdiction, or whether pedagogical practices were the main reasons for more or less successful scores. Rarely was there any examination of the fact that family support or even societal interest might be major factors in test results.

Another indicator of accountability became that of preventing drop-outs, since there was great public concern about the numbers of young people who were not completing high school. Even a cursory examination of the problem revealed that every drop-out was a unique case, that there was no panacea or single solution, although there were common strategies that could help.

Accountable teachers are those who understand their roles, have a grasp of what they wish to teach, are able to reach out to students and address their needs, thereby ensuring that they learn effectively. It seems a simple definition. However, accountable teachers must be constantly learning about themselves and the world that their students will be entering, thereby ensuring that what is taught is always significant.

It's a very tall order, yet there are teachers who regularly go beyond this definition.

Dave Butters

Dave Butters took the concept of accountability to heights of courage and fortitude that defy description. A splendid teacher of physical education in a senior public school, he was struck by cancer of the throat yet continued to teach a subject identified, at least for males, with the necessity of having a voice that will shake the rafters of a normally noisy gymnasium. But despite pain and obvious inconvenience he remained on the job and effective, demonstrating absolute accountability throughout the ups, downs and detours of his professional life.

In the words of his director of education:

> It is a very unusual day indeed not to find
> Mr. Butters in the school gymnasium at 7 a.m.
> He has made the gymnasium at that school
> not only its centre but, to a considerable
> extent, its heart and soul. It is not unusual to
> find 50, 60, or 100 children engaged in
> meaningful activity from dawn until after
> dusk. It is the purposefulness of the activity
> that impresses me most. It is difficult to pick
> Mr. Butters out from the students in a physi-
> cal sense but you know at a glance that a
> master teacher has shaped the behavior of the
> children into the responsible attitudes that are
> expressed. I know personally of young people
> in that school who had become alienated with
> the educational process and, once involved
> with Mr. Butters and his early morning pro-
> grams, have experienced a complete attitude
> reversal.
>
> Now, I know there are lots of teachers in
> the schools who work diligently to prepare
> their lessons, mark the assignments on time,
> and come early or stay late to give added

help, or coaching, or support to the students. Very few, however, are suffering from cancer of the throat and the loss of most of their vocal cords. This, unfortunately, is the case with Mr. Butters. It amazes me that one with so little capacity to be heard manages a gymnasium full of children in a completely orderly and productive way. Dave Butters, in addition to being an outstanding teacher and supporter of young people, is a model of unassuming courage.

Nearly every student who wrote to support Dave's nomination as a Teacher of the Year mentioned his determination to be the best teacher he could be. One of the most poignant comments came from a student who had serious medical problems herself and found inspiration in a teacher also beset by physical difficulties but still carrying out his work with pride, a model of accountability. She wrote:

He has encouraged me to do things I thought I would never be able to do and now I can.
If it wasn't for him, I probably would often be down because a lot of my classmates make fun of me 'cause I can't do as much as they can due to medical problems. I would love to do things they can. But he encouraged me not to worry about what people say — just to do my best. Now I can take more from the people who make fun of me and it doesn't hurt as much.

There are many ways in which a teacher can exhibit accountability. One important way is following up on graduates to see how they have fared. A colleague of Dave's comments on his interest in former students being so intense that he "uses every means available to keep in touch with former students as an interested educator and friend."

In the dedication and commitment of Dave Butters, the term "accountability" takes on new meaning. Throughout his painful rehabilitation treatment he continued to teach successfully, to inspire students, to meet goals. The only change to his career that has been necessary in the last few years, as he nears retirement, has been a shift in program. Dave is no longer in the gymnasium. His loss of vocal function has led him back to the classroom, which puts less strain on his voice. But he still teaches a full day of core subjects — English, history, geography — to his Grade 8 students.

Whatever his teaching assignment, Dave provides constant inspiration. His students call his ability to face challenges, to see each student as different, to keep them all going, "Butter Fever."

As one student put it:

> He's ours, nobody else's. He can't be bought.
> He can't be sold. He's ours 'till the school
> goes bankrupt.

Can there be any greater accolade than to serve a school with such energy and distinction that even students who are not in one's classes remember with pride one's achievements and judge their own success according to one's values? Such is the stuff that heroes are made of, in teaching or, indeed, in any profession.

Carol Shropshire

Carol Shropshire grew up on a dairy farm and attended a one-room rural school. After high school and university she moved to her current school board in a large city where she has worked since 1970. Over the past twenty-four years, she has taught several different primary and junior grades and worked in six schools throughout the board.

While never drifting from her initial school board, Carol Shropshire has tried to change schools every four to five years and change grade levels at the same time. In this way, she forces herself to be open for a new and renewed public and professional scrutiny on a recurring basis. Hence, her levels of accountability can never waver. No wonder her principal remarks on this accountability by noting "her unequivocal belief that all children can learn and that she can teach them."

Carol Shropshire was nominated as Teacher of the Year by a former fellow teacher who, in noting the accountability of her colleague, wrote:

I am now retired but in all my years of teaching, Mrs. Shropshire was the teacher that impressed me the most. She had a wonderful sense of humor and laughed with the children but never let things get out of control. She was an excellent disciplinarian but at no time did a child feel put down by her. She made her students feel important, increasing their own sense of self worth from the slowest to the brightest.

She had the most thorough tracking system so that each child completed everything that was assigned and no child fell through the cracks. Not only was work completed but all corrections were made down to the last "i" being dotted and "t" being crossed. Spelling and Math were corrected. Any work not completed in school was worked on from 3:30 to 4:00. No child or parent complained. They were all grateful for her individual concern and attention.

Her lessons were thoroughly prepared and so interestingly presented that a child could not help but learn. I always felt that every teacher in training should have to spend a month in her classroom and then our system would have the best trained teachers in Canada.

Tim Willis

Tim Willis spent his seventh birthday on board a ship dodging bombs in the North Atlantic en route to Canada from Britain in 1940. He came with his mother and three older brothers. Upon arrival, the family were billetted in different homes. The family was not reunited until they all returned to Britain in 1945 when Tim was twelve years old.

Between 1951 and 1953, Tim served with the Royal Navy and in the mid-1950s, he returned to Canada in style. He came to deliver a boat-load of cattle and pigs. And this time, he came to stay.

After immigrating, Tim completed an apprenticeship in mechanics, but in the early 1960s he became a teacher and began a new career at his first school, in a small town. He has remained there since.

As automotive teacher and director of the technical department, Tim has added an extra R to the traditional 3Rs — Responsibility. His students learn more than Reading, Riting and Rithmetic, they learn to repair, build, maintain and design the tools of their futures — tractors, jeeps, buses, cars. Tim's sense of responsibility — or accountability — to the community and to his students' future was brought to light by a colleague, a science teacher who wrote:

> Our population is rural and our population levels are the same as those in the early 1960s when changes were introduced into rural high schools to make them fully composite rather than academic. Our young are an export. And the technical careers for our graduates sometimes have been unnoticed and unresolved. The economic payback for our area must be high also, since most of the carpenters, automechanics and electricians in our school are now our graduates. Mr. Willis has played an important role in the success of technical education.
>
> The automotive shops developed by Tim Willis have an excellent collection of diesel engines as well as the usual gas ones. A diesel program is of particular benefit to our rural area. Tim's diesels range from Caterpillar D8 and D2, Cummings, Perkins, to a water-cooled didster marine diesel. I can remember very well the day a wrecker arrived from Kitchener bearing a Detroit Diesel. An ex-student had remembered Tim's request to have one someday. And so, the Detroit arrived without warning.
>
> At least two of Tim's students have become Technical Teachers after apprenticeship while many of those that returned to farming first became confident about fixing tractors and

machinery in Tim's classes. (An ability to maintain machinery yourself and to keep it going for many years is essential to survival in these hard economic times on the farm.)

Our school board owns some of its own school buses. Tim and his students maintain the spare bus assigned to our school for field trip use. I am sure you would agree that such a bus is a valuable addition to any school program.

This past fall, Tim and students have adopted a wrecked Jeep for shop use. Tim obtained the Jeep as a donation from Chrysler.

Tim Willis continually takes his responsibility to rural life beyond the school and thus continually integrates school knowledge with the real world. In this regard his students have the advantage of applied knowledge and thus have an automatic link to the world beyond the school.

His former principal has described his contribution in the following words:

I have known Tim as a colleague in teaching since he started in 1963 until the present. During all these years he has had only one prime purpose in teaching and that is the "student."

In his field of auto mechanics he has had to live within strict budget restrictions so he would spend hours of his personal time to get teaching aids at little or no cost and then fix them to be used in the classroom. One example of this is a large diesel engine which was damaged and available at no cost. He was able to find used parts to get it working for a teaching engine...

Mr. Willis has always been unselfish of his time. He takes upgrading courses in his summer holidays. He serves on committees within his own federation, he has served terms on the local town council and parks board. He works in placing his students in the work force both for work experience and upon graduation. He keeps a close liaison with the local tradesmen and spends time visiting his students on the job.

He is a student's teacher in that he uses his subject as an instrument to teach students how to survive in everyday life and teaches them to "get their hands dirty."

Educational systems, especially in Canada, have not been kind to teachers whose genius has been that of attending to the skills of the hand as well as those of the mind. Some countries, wisely, have given more support to polytechnics. Unfortunately, in many schools, the shop wing continues to be the place where the perceived dull or recalcitrant student can be consigned with the least negative effect. The impact of this attitude can be seen as we confront a technological age that requires engineers and technicians. Our world will need many Tim Willises if we are to meet the challenge of a society that demands excellence in the practical as well as the theoretical.

Anne Hummel

In her community, Anne Hummel is known by the name of the school, "Mrs. Rosebank." She lives a minute's walking distance from the school that she has taught at for the majority of her teaching career and she is often on its premises during off-hours and summer holidays. As a result, her accountability both on and off the job is constant. She may leave the job for a few hours here or there but the job never leaves her.

About the commitment of this hard-working teacher, her principal and colleagues say that she is determined to be the best that she can be. Whether with her own students or those of others, she is always a teacher, never missing the opportunity to contribute to learning or to share information. Her own personal books are in constant circulation and she shares willingly both services and materials.

Anne Hummel is more than accountable; she is second-generation accountable. She has taught children of her original students and her continued exuberance speaks to her commitment to service.

In teaching, testing of students yields too little evidence of real educational outcomes to justify extensive and expensive screening. For in fact, no measure of accountability equals the living proof — that is, a student who has succeeded, and who knows where to lay the credit. For Anne Hummel this accolade of accountability came in double measure.

She was nominated as Teacher of the Year by a former student who is now a policeman and the parent of one of Anne Hummel's current students.

He wrote:

Back to school, Grade 5, 1967. There were new friendships and new challenges for young, pre-pubescent minds, and a new teacher... Miss Pisani.

It was love at first sight!

She was a young, beautiful, fireball of energy, and she was enjoying her first permanent teaching assignment at William G. Miller Public School in West Hill, Ontario.

... and she was all mine! (well, for the year anyway).

Now don't get me wrong. There were other girls of course. I mean... at that age, hormones doing what they do and all, I think I was in love just about every other week with just about every other girl. It was nature's "roller coaster ride through hell and back," for some further benefit I guess.

Through all of this "confusion" I was soon to realize that all I could seriously hope to have with her though was a simple student/teacher relationship... just like everyone else.

Life sucked!

Well... I wasn't about to let this minor set-back destroy me. I promised myself that I'd do the one and only thing that was right. I'd do my best for her. I'd be a model student; a class act to follow... I'd be a shining example of her most generous tutelage.

I blew it!

Just how many times I got into trouble that year, I can't remember. It seemed that my desk and I were segregated from the rest of the class so often that I actually began to enjoy the privacy...

Then there was the day I made her lose her voice while giving me a much deserved blast. It dropped off sharply and, in a squeaky, gaspy kind of way, just disappeared...

Her enthusiastic approach, and excellent teaching skills got me by for another year. Such dedication to duty demands some recognition for sure.

She stayed on as a teacher. I later finished school and went on to become a police officer in the Big City.

There she was, busy at her end, dishing out those things that give people in this life a fighting chance. Things like knowledge, pride, self-esteem and hope.

I was busy at the other end, most often dealing with those that had gotten off track, those who had given up on all of those things that she had worked so hard to instill.

Funny how that happens ...

And it's funny how, many years later, I would come to settle down with my wife (it was love at first sight!) and children in a small Pickering neighborhood, with a small elementary school just like the one I used to go to. And it's funny how one of the teachers on staff there would just happen to be...

There **SHE** was! **MY** grade 5 teacher!

I think I've got an idea now, what part of that "roller coaster ride" was all about. I'm able to look upon this woman with a great deal of respect and admiration... for what she gave me, and for what she has probably given so many other kids over the years.

Nature must have taken its toll on her too. She says she can't remember me being the little shit that I was, and tells my kids that I was one of her best students.

Too kind!

Mrs. Anne Hummel of Rosebank Road Public School (Pickering) enjoyed her 25th year in teaching last year. A Silver Anniversary! I know, she reminded me enough. She kept asking me what "we" were going to do to celebrate the occasion. I promised that we'd do "something."

I blew it! (Again)

I have to figure that just sending my kids off to her school won't cut it. It's not nearly enough. She deserves better.

This wonderful woman still harbors all those fine traits and qualities, that she had when she came into my life so long ago (if not more so). She's one of those unsung heroes (or is it heroines?) that one hears about, for all that she is, and all she has done, and oh yes, she is a loyal Blue Jay Fan!

I think it's about time I let go and shared MY TEACHER with the rest of the World.

Donna Ross

Donna Ross is a teacher's teacher. She quite simply loves the job. She has spent more than thirty years in the same profession, at the same school, for the same board of education, yet her enthusiasm is still infectious, her energy and spirit undiminished.

In educational terms, Donna is a grandmother; like Anne Hummel, she is now teaching the children of her former students. In fact, the caretaker at her present school was in her Grade 1 class years ago.

As an elementary teacher, Donna is part of the meat and potatoes of schooling. Without these foundations, we would never learn or even want to learn: these years are the grass roots of education and they form the essence of accountability. If the education system fails early in learning, the total investment is jeopardized.

Donna Ross began teaching at the age of eighteen and has seen her school area grow from a township to a borough and, finally, to a city. Over her two generations of teaching time, she has remained committed and forever answerable to her children, their families and her colleagues. Her professional longevity, the uninterrupted smooth flow of her career, bears witness to the ultimate demonstration of accountability.

And her level of performance has never diminished. In 1990 she was a member of a team of three that won the Marshall McLuhan Distinguished Teacher Award for their work in bringing technology into the classroom in a meaningful way. In 1991, the very next year, she was selected as a Teacher of the Year. She is still going as strong as ever.

Donna was nominated by her sister, who wrote:

> Donna Ross is one of the most outstanding teachers anywhere. She is truly dedicated to the craft of teaching. She gives the art of teaching a new dimension because of her knowledge, skill, humor, empathy, fairness, honesty, intelligence and her deep sense of caring for her pupils, their families, the community and her colleagues. Donna is a persistent optimist who is always "up."
>
> When asked for an idea or solution to almost any problem, Donna can deliver at

least six good ideas on the spot. She is aware of and concerned for the world around her. Fairness, either seen or perceived, is deep within the very fibre of her being. She cannot tolerate unfairness in any situation. She is willing to speak her mind whenever she meets prejudice, unfairness, cruelty (physical or mental), stupidity, or just plain thoughtlessness. She speaks her mind, but always with fairness and caring.

SUMMARY

There is a common suspicion that teachers somehow resent being accountable for their actions, their effectiveness, their performance. Great teachers have no hesitation about being responsible for what happens in their classrooms. However, they may legitimately question, "Accountable? To whom? For what?"

With all the inconsistencies and distortions in the field it is unreasonable to hold our teachers accountable for students' performances on international tests if, in fact, teachers are being asked to prepare students to excel in a lot of areas that have little reference to the subject matter being tested. Indeed, that kind of accountability is no accountability at all.

If, however, teachers like Dave Butters, Carol Shropshire, Tim Willis, Anne Hummel and Donna Ross are to be held accountable for the learning that is appropriate to the expectations of society and the capacities and motivational strengths of their students, none of them would argue that this isn't fair.

A wise teacher knows exactly what constitutes accountability regardless of the false promises of standardized testing or group standards that create fear of being found wanting and the paralysis of creativity and caring that such terror carries with it.

CHAPTER 7

The Relevant Teacher

In today's economy, success in education is being measured in very concrete terms — namely, a job. In essence, the public is demanding practical, measurable proof of school success:

Will this student be employable?

When the economy is flourishing, learning is not focussed totally on the marketplace. With rampant unemployment, however, parents expect education to be job-focussed. The underlying question, "Is my child being prepared for the future?" is what precipitates every outcry to re-examine programs, cut frills and get back to basics.

With the name of the educational game being future employment, it is obviously time to establish more than abstract links to the world outside the classroom. Business and industry will not want our students unless they fit current needs.

Yet, ironically, teachers are faced with the new reality that today's students may not be entering a world of full employment. Technological advances have destroyed hundreds of thousands of jobs. Corporations and government ministries and agencies are "right-sizing," a euphemism for laying off or early-retiring armies of employees. This policy continues even in the face of an expected upturn in the economy. And part-time work is replacing many full-time jobs with all the disadvantages to workers whose social service nets and pensions are reduced.

Thus, teachers have the almost impossible task of providing a relevant educational experience preparing young people for what may be a limited but still existing opportunity for employment, while also simultaneously teaching them to be self-sufficient, imaginative and flexible during the times they will have to sustain themselves through their own wit and energy.

Even more complex is the task of teachers who must determine what characteristics may enhance students' capacity to be employees, self-sustaining, or both. Very often employers are seeking skills, knowledge, attitudes and habits that are more relevant to the '70s or '80s, although there is every indication that creativity, imagination, cooperative skills and critical thinking capacity will be the attributes most necessary to survive in the future. For example, employers — and parents — frequently demand more science, math and technology, when in fact a balance of these subjects with physical education, music, drama, visual arts or literature may well be more useful in the years to come.

For these reasons a relevant teacher must become both a guide and an interpreter, helping students become aware of the world beyond the school. In other words, the teacher must facilitate the move from here to there, from blackboard to boardroom, from today to tomorrow.

In our study of top teachers, these aspects of relevance were stressed over and over again by students. Regardless of subject area or grade, students admire teachers who do more than describe the real world; they are part of it. In fact, favorite teachers, and those judged to be the best in the profession, were often found to be people who have held other jobs, people who do more than translate, people who understand. They have the credibility to lead their students into the workplace.

The relevant teacher, as a result, more than anyone else, has the power to reverse the drop-out syndrome. These teachers understand, identify and empathize. In fact, many were drop-outs themselves en route from student to teacher, drop-outs by traditional definitions, but star models to follow by living example.

Ian Barrett

Ian Barrett is a man for all seasons, all terrains, all school subjects, all sports and all interests. Few people can ever hope to approach his levels of versatility and achievement.

He has studied biochemistry, accounting, law and computers, has taught math, physics and biology. He has coached basketball, lacrosse, hockey and football. He set up an outdoor education program for his board in the early 1970s that was the first of its type in North America and for the past twenty years has continued to serve as a model.

When Ian Barrett began the outdoor education project at his inner-city high school, he felt that it was an ideal place to begin the job of building the self-image of potential drop-outs. He was working at a school with alarming social statistics and a reputation for violence and poor achievement. The program, Ian reasoned, would be good for both the students and the school, turning unattractive and boring into exciting and enticing.

Few of the students he began the program with had ever left the concrete jungle, let alone experienced nature close up. Ian Barrett organized the entire Grade 10 student body and outfitted them with tents, sleeping bags, food, clothes, cooking utensils, staff support and activities for a week of camping and learning.

Barrett's colleagues were amazed at his energy and zeal. He managed to excite fellow staff members enough that they joined the project, but the major job of pulling together the program was his and most of the work was done on his own time without any adjustment in his regular timetable. It is fully to his credit that well over 3,000 students have now participated in his board's outdoor education program and the school has seen a significant reduction in drop-outs and an increase in parental involvement as a result.

A large number of the students who participate in Ian's program are immigrants, and for them, with limited or no English language skills, it has provided a unique opportunity "to assimilate rapidly into the school and local environment and to feel welcomed and comfortable, rough-hewn, true-blue, Canadians."

No wonder that education systems worldwide have followed this model and its highly relevant approach to common problems.

The initiation of the outdoor education project was not Ian Barrett's only effort to keep education relevant. When some of his students came to him to plead for help with photography, he turned their interest into courses with credits. He even began to teach photography full-time and his students have won several high school competitions.

Always a role model, Ian now works successfully as a professional photographer and by personal example encourages his students to form relevant link-ups with the community.

His nominator, a colleague, says of this unbeatable choice for Teacher of the Year:

> What is truly amazing about Ian Barrett is that these two nationally recognized programs, Outdoor Education and Photography, barely touch the surface of his contribution to education. He initiated the first Yearbook Co-Op to allow students to learn all aspects of book production from design, to artwork, photography, typesetting and marketing. He computerized the school accounts and then established a student-run accounts system whereby all school financial transactions are recorded (under his supervision) by students — with a full printout and analysis. This further involves students in the life of the school and teaches them actual skills for business. Ian has also introduced a regular series of community newsletters that are produced by students on a desktop publisher and run off on school presses by students. Ian is presently one of four teachers introducing AT & T's "Classroom of Tomorrow" concept which allows instant communication via satellite with schools in six other countries — once again, Ian is at the leading edge of the future of education. He was a pioneer in Educational Travel, taking his students to 14 different countries. He has given more than 50 workshops to other teachers and student groups on Outdoor Education planning, Organizational Development for High School Teachers, and Teachers and the Law. He has written seven books and resource guides for use in high schools on topics ranging from Organic Chemistry for High School Students, to Outdoor Education guides to The Legal Maze.

He is presently writing a book on Photography for students. Ian's enormous energy is further illustrated by the fact that he has been actively involved in coaching for 21 years. He established the lacrosse league and the hockey league to provide outlets for students that were not then available. He coached 26 teams in lacrosse, basketball, football, hockey and volleyball to 21 championship games. He took his hockey team on a tour of the Soviet Union in 1972.

Ian has had a greater impact on the educational system at our school than any other teacher. The community now believes that their school is the best and unlike the old days when bail-out was occurring, when students were leaving for perceived violence and lack of educational achievement, many students are now transferring in, especially for Outdoor Education and Photography.

Myles Crawford

A teacher in the arts in our schools, whether it be drama, visual arts or music, faces a peculiar challenge. The arts have obvious attractions for many students who see their entertainment idols singing and dancing on stage or acting on television. However, there is also a deeply held belief that such subjects are not relevant, are indeed peripheral at best to the serious task of being schooled for the working world. At worst the arts are seen as trivial and unworthy of any attention. In these days of emphasis on the economy, activities outside what is deemed the central core curriculum or the "basics" are assumed to be of little importance in the essential process of preparing young people for the reality of employment.

Myles Crawford, a teacher of music in an urban secondary school, was selected as a Teacher of the Year for reasons that had nothing to do with the entertainment or amusement of his students and everything to do with relevance and outcome. The arts, in his hands, deal with student learning, self-realization and preparation for living in an information society. One parent put it succinctly: "His main focus has always been to help kids learn." And of course, students do learn many things through the arts — indeed, for some, the arts are at times the only route to learning.

Myles Crawford's school principal referred to him as "dynamic, talented, student-centred," and emphasized the enormous commitment he was prepared to make to the extra-curricular program. To some extent, after-school and early morning rehearsals go with the territory of teaching in the performing arts. However, it is clear that this is an extraordinary professional who challenges both himself and his students to achieve the highest level of performance. His stage band represented all of southern Ontario in the National Championships after it had already taken first place in the local Kiwanis Music Festival.

But it was much more than an expanded after-hours commitment that led his students to support his nomination for a Teacher of the Year Award. They stressed his continuing demand for excellence that transcended mere competition with other musical ensembles. It is evident to both students and their parents that he stretches their capabilities both individually and collectively and does so with a unique combination of demanding leadership and playful encouragement.

One parent describes his style as "always building up their self-confidence and helping them to push themselves for that extra note... to take that extra step... with a right mixture of fun, friendship and discipline."

The debate on school effectiveness has tended to focus on standards that are measurable along with a process of rigorous testing that supposedly assures quality in the classroom. It is sometimes forgotten that an outstanding teacher is a constant example of excellence, one that emerges from the values and commitment of the individual. Myles imbues his students with a feeling of personal responsibility for excellence that can be transferred from trumpet to pen, from trombone to computer, from flute to the most sophisticated technology.

Parents remark upon the way Crawford uses community resources. He and his students haunt concert halls, theatres and, perhaps surprisingly, jazz clubs. Crawford believes that students can learn from watching professionals at work. If students are to achieve they must witness and emulate the true professional, in this case, the musician. There is no substitute for studying a person in the workplace who must perform with energy and commitment every minute on-stage, Crawford believes.

This teacher stands out because he recognizes that quality learning can take place outside the classroom. He is prepared to convince both students and their parents that this is a legitimate learning experience.

A high drop-out rate is seen as a school's failure to serve the needs of many children and young people. There have been proposals suggesting that every student should have a mentor who can follow the progress of that student and be a constant source of caring, comfort, encouragement, challenge and advice. There have always been teachers like Myles prepared to go beyond the limits of the job description or particular curriculum expertise to recognize a human connection that transcends the formal teacher-student relationship and brings lifelong relevance to today's teaching, as described in his letter of nomination:

> Mr. Crawford is one of those teachers that is totally dedicated to helping kids, 24 hours a day, 7 days a week. Regardless of the time of day, regardless of whether their problem is with music, homework or a personal problem all of Mr. Crawford's kids are free to call him for help and they all do. He has become their friend not just their teacher.
>
> I never worry about what my kid is doing because most of the time that he goes to concerts or other trips with the school, Mr. Crawford is there making sure that all the kids are safe. He gives his whole heart and soul to his kids.
>
> Mr. Crawford is not only fully dedicated to the kids but he treats them as adults. If Mr. Crawford asked any of the kids or their parents to jump we would all say, How high?
>
> I think that you will not find a better role model for our kids or for other teachers in all of Canada. Please vote Mr. Crawford Teacher of the Year.

Myles is a competent, knowledgeable professional musician, one who could make his living on-stage or in the orchestra pit. In his acceptance speech for the Teacher of the Year Award he admitted that during these years of teacher-bashing he has sometimes identified himself as a musician. However, in the light of this honor, he assured colleagues, parents and students that he would proudly be a teacher in the future.

Myles Crawford takes risks, which is the challenge of the teacher who seeks to be relevant. Often the traditional and the tried must be forsaken, and the new and experimental sought out, leaving some students and parents feeling uneasy and uncomfortable. The career of Myles Crawford attests to the fact that a life of courage and risk can be explained and justified to both students and their parents — indeed, that such behavior can become a source of pride for all associated with learning.

Marlene Anderson

Marlene Anderson was not always a teacher. Her first jobs included working as a secretary, a dental assistant and a model. One day, while she was giving a grooming course in a high school, a teacher told her, "You should be a teacher. You're a natural." Not long afterwards, Marlene began her teaching career on a temporary basis. She was unqualified but there was a major teacher shortage and she was hired to help fill the gap by teaching business subjects. Determined not to give up her new career, she began to upgrade her qualifications. While teaching full-time and raising her own two children, she completed four degrees at university (B.A., B.Ed., M.Ed., Ed.D.), all with first-class honors. And while she was studying, Marlene began to investigate one of her major concerns as a teacher — student suicide. She ultimately based her doctoral dissertation on the subject of education about death. After completing her doctorate in education, Marlene once again amazed her colleagues and students. She went back to school, this time to complete an MBA in Michigan, again while teaching full-time. Her commitment to education, her own and her students, is obvious in her own achievement. Her students consider her a role model in her fight for equal opportunity. Throughout her career, Marlene has been particularly careful to make young women around her aware of the need to watch the world around them when planning their education. Times change and only people who adapt to the changes survive and thrive. One critical area that she has stressed in her teaching is the particular need for female students to acquire strong skills in mathematics and science and to become qualified for positions of technical and business responsibility.

Marlene teaches that education transcends the school classroom. She believes that curriculum should be "world-based" and although she lives and works in a small northern city, she lets no geographical boundary limit her quest for knowledge or relevance to her work. Her own studies have involved travel and the result has been that her students have learned by watching her that education is universal and ongoing.

Marlene explains her role in education as one in which she assists students to assimilate, analyse and synthesize facts, and thereby helps each student become more able to achieve the maximum of his or her potential. Students say that because of her attitude and manner with the students in her classes, each one is assured that learning will occur in an atmosphere of caring and support.

Marlene now has over twenty-five years of teaching experience. For the past ten years she has been director of business studies at her school.

Her dream of a broader-based curriculum has been realized in her involvement with her school board's Directions 2000 project. As we head towards the next century, Marlene works to gather input from all segments of the larger community on how schools must adapt to remain relevant in the coming years.

Her principal calls her competent and innovative and very knowledgeable about the latest trends and technologies.

One of her students supported these thoughts in her letter of nomination:

> Because Dr. Anderson has maintained a
> strong link with the business world through
> Co-Operative Education liaisons and her
> advanced studies, a more managed approach
> to curriculum development and implementa-
> tion has been seen in her classrooms. Each
> course that I have studied with Dr. Anderson
> has indicated vital, improved techniques. She

has never taught the same course in the same manner in the twenty-four years she has taught — because there have always been some new methods which will make our studies more pertinent to the outside world. The content of the class assignments indicate that we must become more politically-conscious, consumer-orientated, and aware of the specific concerns of our society.

In addition to the philosophy of education and society which we have learned from Dr. Anderson, we are also proud of her accomplishments in acquiring her own qualifications, and her leadership qualities which are applied within our school and our community.

Dr. Anderson is an energetic, effective worker, and has provided her assistance to the Business Educators Association as an area councillor, and is a member of the Business and Professional Women's Club, the Business Directors' Association, the Alpha Delta Kappa Educators' Sorority and the Women Educational Administrators.

As a student I am also familiar with the love and devotion she shows to her children and two grandchildren — whose photographs are all over her bulletin board in her office. Her hobbies of watercolor, oil and acrylic painting and weaving, knitting, needlework, reading, musical appreciation, and hiking with her dogs keep her well physically and emotionally.

The years which she spent in industry before coming to teaching have been mentioned in her classes whenever her own personal business experience can be applied to the subject content. Because of this real world experience, we feel that our training is more practical and valuable.

Because of her dedication to her students and her position, and because of the example as a role model which she offers to each of

her students — I truly believe that Dr.
Anderson is deserving of the selection as
Teacher Of The Year.

Educational systems have a reputation for being unconnected to the work of business and industry. There must be more teachers like Marlene Anderson who are comfortable in the community — and more community members who can address tasks in the school. Only in the positive interaction of teachers and community leaders from business, trade unions and voluntary associations, can effective cooperation be forged to the benefit of our schools and our society. Partnership, not isolation, is the keyword for the future.

Marjorie Fonck

For young children the atmosphere of the classroom itself can determine whether students see any relevance in what they study. If a child feels comfortable, then what transpires in class becomes an adventure of the spirit and mind. If the child senses that threat and embarrassment will be important components of learning at school, then education takes on a negative aura, perhaps never to become the source of joy, excitement and fulfilment we would like it to be for every person.

Marjorie Fonck's nominator describes her impact vividly:

> Recognizing the effect that the classroom
> environment has on the life and development
> of the primary child, she strives to create an
> ideal environment where children can develop
> to their fullest potential in all areas, and each
> one can emerge happy, unique, confident and
> beautiful with a love of learning, a positive
> self-concept and a responsible and caring
> feeling toward others.

Perhaps her greatest contribution is her understanding of the relevance of "play." The word has lost its lustre in recent years, when preparation for work has become the focus of our educational institutions.

It is ironic that during the '60s there were countless workshops on how we were to cope with the leisure society in the wake of cybernation and its effects on the workplace. Now we know that, for a host of reasons, families have less "play time" — or discretionary time for leisure — than in those halcyon years following the Second World War. Thus, learning to play and learning through play have received less attention.

Then, of course, there is the effect of television. Certainly no other invention has so revolutionized the way both children and adults use their leisure time. In affluent North America the availability of a huge selection of channels has lured children to an unparallelled degree to the pervasive presence of the TV screen. One statistic appears again and again: the success of children in school is affected dramatically, and negatively, by the amount of television they watch. Teachers are conscious of the effect of television on attention span, active curiosity and physical energy every day of their professional lives.

Television has had one effect on the children of the last quarter of the 20th century — it has made them more passive in their play. There are those who claim that it undermines the natural imagination and creativity that spring from young minds. But Marjorie Fonck's students have an advantage:

> Her children love to learn. They truly think of work as play and play as work.

Marjorie sees her role as that of teaching in such a way that reading, maths and science are so exciting that the distance between work and play dissolves. And her commitment is to the long term.

Her principal observes:

> As a teacher at Ossington/Old Orchard Public School, she has produced two generations of children who love to learn. Parents are on lengthy waiting lists to have their children in her program. During the past 8 years she has inspired both fellow teachers and administrators.

One of the great advantages of giving parents more choice in the schools to which they can send their children as opposed to limiting attendance to the schools in their own district, is the fact that teachers like Marjorie Fonck are recognized and sought out by those who care most about their children and their learning.

As well, Fonck's fame as a teacher has gone beyond the school and its clientele. National television has highlighted her ideas and her hands-on experience of play in a program titled "The Serious Business of Play." The impact of that exposure has been felt across the school system.

One of the most progressive faculties of education has made every effort to engage Marjorie Fonck as a full-time professor. She continues to give of her talent on a part-time basis. Her true commitment is to the classroom and the children she loves so much.

> Visitors have come from all over North
> America to see her program... Subjects such
> as reading, story writing, math and science
> activities are often the first choice of the child.
> We are fortunate to have such a teacher who
> has been so inspirational to both her pupils
> and fellow teachers. She truly is the epitome
> of a gifted educator.

At the end of the day, the most important contribution any teacher can make to the future well-being of a student must be that of instilling a love of learning and some strategies whereby every student can learn what needs to be known. Marjorie Fonck has captured the way to create a lifelong learner who can bring joy and satisfaction both to self and to others.

Bert Oussoren

Some teachers stay in one school for decades because it fulfils their desire to serve in a particular way.

Bert Oussoren moved from the Netherlands to New Jersey, then on to Vancouver and Manitoba before he settled in Kenora, a small isolated northern Ontario town. He had taught there for twenty-six years at the time of his nomination.

He has an insatiable curiosity about other lands and other people. He sees it as part of his relevance as a geography teacher. However, it is not enough just to inform his students about the Rocky Mountains — he believes it is his duty to ensure they experience the awe-inspiring peaks with their own eyes.

Having travelled the world himself, he is determined that his students share this enthusiasm.

His principal describes his role:

> Mr. Oussoren has come to be known in the community as the teacher who has done more than any other to ensure that students have an opportunity to travel abroad. Given that Kenora is located in central Canada and students by and large have few opportunities for travel, Mr. Oussoren's program has been particularly appreciated. It has been in place for 22 years and has given hundreds of students the opportunity to visit cultures that they would not normally have seen.

The future will witness an increasing mixture of cultures, languages and colors, and the students of this remote town will be able to cope with this multicultural explosion because of the tenacity of their geography teacher. Each trip is preceded by an educational program preparing these students for the experience ahead as they visit large cities in foreign lands that are beyond the imagination of many of them.

Travelling the world may well be a part of life for many of these young people. But community service will even more likely be a source of personal satisfaction. Bert Oussoren has headed the Honor Society at his school. This group of students does community service on behalf of the voluntary sector — in this case, the Salvation Army, and in each of the past four years the students have hosted a dinner for seniors. Not only is the event organized by the Honor Society but its members serve the supper and provide entertainment. If the future well-being of our communities must involve activities which bring joy and satisfaction to the most vulnerable, then Bert Oussoren is preparing his students well for their after-school life.

Bert's role as guidance teacher was stressed by Frank Miclash, a former student, a former colleague as a teacher in his school and now an elected member of the provincial legislature.

As a high school student I encountered the many problems and challenges of growing up which are universally shared by young people. My grades were average and I plodded along with no real goal in mind and absolutely nothing in sight as far as my future.

Upon entering Grade 13 (now OAC) it became evident that there were other things that might be of more interest to me than school. I had just completed a fairly successful summer working in the field of leasing product sales and come October I decided that earning money was more appealing than furthering my education. Thus, I left school to pursue this sales career. Leasing product sales got slow later in the winter and I moved from sales to automobile sales at a local dealership.

I can remember now that beautiful day in May when I was gazing out the window of the automobile showroom contemplating my future. It was almost like out of nowhere that Mr. Oussoren appeared. We got into a discussion about my future and to this day I can remember him saying, 'Frank, you can always come back to selling cars but furthering your education will only open other doors for you in the future.'

Even though I did not sell this very special person a car, I did find myself back at Beaver Brae Secondary School in September for the best year both academically and socially, that I ever had throughout my entire school years.

From here it was on to the University of Manitoba from which I graduated with a B.A. and Certification in Education. During my student teaching days the University allowed me to return to Kenora to train with Mr. Oussoren. Of course, he was a geography teacher and my major had somehow become geography. He truly was an exceptional teacher in this area and sparked interest in all who took his class.

Mr. Oussoren's dedication to helping young people is something which I and hundreds of students throughout the Kenora area shall not forget. His classes were always interesting and challenging. His involvements in extra-curricular activities including the organization of an annual trip to some far off country are numerous. My first trip to Europe and my appetite for travel were all a result of his efforts.

By the way, I ended up coming back to the Kenora Board of Education to teach and even-tually became the attendance counsellor. This gave me many opportunities to relay the wise advice Mr. Oussoren had given to me.

The people of this small town have reason to celebrate the fact that a man like Bert Oussoren has chosen to do his lifework in their community.

SUMMARY

It is difficult to cope with the multi-faceted concept of relevance. Teachers are faced with a fast-changing world. The regular cur-riculum becomes dated as soon as it is written. What is relevant today may be irrelevant tomorrow. Teachers are challenged to think about the future in the knowledge that their students will probably face a very different set of personal and societal prob-lems than those of the past, perhaps focussed on environmen-tal sustainability rather than the consumption of goods and services, on the broad distribution of well-being rather than on the creation of affluence in the shadow of planetary poverty.

In this context, relevance becomes a significant measure of the intellectual stature and spiritual reach of the great teacher.

CHAPTER 8

Beyond Standards

In most definitions, our understanding of a teacher stems from the verb, "to teach." After all, the verb, the action word, says it all — teaching is the *giving* of information, *inducing* by example, the process of *enabling* someone to do something through instruction or training.

The job, by definition, is active.

But then, so is learning.

Just as does each teacher, so does each student bring certain competencies to the learning situation, certain strengths, weaknesses, previous knowledge, missing information, prejudices and fears.

No teacher or student approaches the complex challenges of learning in quite the same way. While some learning experiences are welcome surprises, too many others are mere exercises in self-fulfilling prophecies of failure.

The reasons for the failures of students have been thoroughly investigated over the past few decades. Under-achievement due to negative family factors, peer pressure and poverty has been well-documented.

We all know that the student with the best educational prognosis comes to school intact physically, mentally, behaviorally and socially.

The role of the teacher in success or failure has been less fully explored, the role of the relationship between teacher and student almost ignored.

But we all know that not all educational marriages are successful. Only some manage to reach the levels of communication and respect that are common to Teachers of the Year, such as Lorraine

Bain, described by a grateful parent:

> I struggled to hold back the tears. He just
> wanted to sing with the rest of the children in
> the play. But he was unable to control his
> own behavior. He was jumping all over the
> benches as the rest of the children sat quietly
> awaiting their turn to perform. I watched Mrs.
> Bain, she waited as long as she could before
> she had to remove him from the performance.
> When she did she took him very quietly,
> placed him on her lap, and very patiently
> calmed him down.
> I learned very quickly how much love and
> care this woman had in her heart not only for
> my son but every single child in her class.
> You know they will leave her class with
> exactly what she wanted to teach them.

At its best, teaching is an unbeatable profession. Blessed with the "forever effect," a good teacher is often remembered long after friends and colleagues are forgotten.

The following words were written by an "old boy," fourteen years after leaving high school, about his former rugby coach and teacher, Red Lipsett:

> One thing that Red has shared with one and
> all is that, at least once, he has taken the
> time, just to talk and ask how, or what, we
> were doing. This feeling of caring is the driving
> force behind so many of us returning year
> after year to enjoy ourselves and say thanks to
> the "Red Man."

The original intention of the Teacher of the Year contest was to provide successful students with a way to say thank you to the teachers who had made their successes possible. Thousands of thank-you letters described thousands of teachers who taste success regularly. The byproduct of these accolades became the data for this book.

The letters, as readers will no doubt have noticed, were from the heart, but written with careful thought. People know what they like in teachers but, most importantly, they are sure of what works.

Through their participation, they have made this book possible. They are in effect co-authors and their contribution is acknowledged with gratitude. They took the valuable time and made the important effort without promises of rewards, recognition — or better grades.

While many glowing reviews came from parents and colleagues, the student perspective was especially interesting. The students who wrote were consistent in their preferences among teachers. To gain a vote as one of the best, a teacher is typically appreciated for behavior that includes:

1. extending instructional time until the lesson is fully understood — that is, taking the extra time needed to help a student learn;
2. caring about the students' feelings, treating each student as a person (at the secondary level, superior teachers are those who know all the students in a class by name); and
3. dressing well.

In other words, the ideal teacher, the cream of the teacher crop, according to this sample of consumer opinion, is a person who is intent on teaching, who acts at all times like a human being — and who tries to look attractive!

There can be no doubt that the teaching profession needs a few public pats on the back. The front line in education is vulnerable because it receives too little positive feedback from too few people. And pats on the back and votes of confidence, especially when offered spontaneously, eloquently and openly, as they are for Teachers of the Year, are vital, whether they come from parents, colleagues or students.

Re: Barbara Hruska, a teacher nearing retirement:

> I knew the first morning in September that
> she was a winner. She told us she was 19.
> Actually she has two grown children. Also,
> she said the initial "B" in her name stood for
> 'Beautiful', instead of Barbara. What a great
> way to start off a brand new school year. My
> class and I loved her from the beginning.

Re: Alexander Sheel, a high school French teacher:

We all learned to think, read and talk French better than ever before. He's got guts and he knows what it takes to motivate an under-achiever or to continue to captivate those of us who are excelling in modern languages.

It's a great feeling when you can say that you have learned a lot in a class, while having fun doing it, from a devoted teacher who loves his work and therefore makes others love to learn.

Re: Marlene Phillips, from Australia, with thirty years of teaching experience:

Marlene Phillips is recognized by both parents and peers as being an outstanding teacher. Despite the fact that she is nearing retirement, Marlene shows no signs at all of slowing the pace. I do not exaggerate in the least when I tell you that she arrives at school shortly after seven in the morning and very often works until seven or eight in the evening. I would estimate that on average she works a ten hour day. The fact that she has for years been affec-tionately referred to by her colleagues as the "roadrunner" should give you some idea of how much energy she has — combine that with a nice sense of humor, excellent rapport with staff and children, excellent teaching ability, great organizaitonal skills and what you have, as previously stated, is an outstand-ing teacher.

Re: Joseph Hocevar, a quiet-spoken veteran of the front line:

Mr. Hocevar is a parent's dream because they see that not only is he building a solid math foundation but that students actually enjoy math classes. He also prepares students for

logical thinking, planning and problem
solving. He commands respect, but not fear.

Re: William Squirrell, the founder of his rural school's Outer
Club:

> Mr. Squirrell believes all students can learn
> and sets very high expectation levels for
> achievement. He believes in a cooperative
> learning process where people only get out of
> teaching and learning what you put into it.

Re: Jeannette Wilson, an elementary music teacher:

> When the try-outs for the band were held,
> Brian was so nervous that he couldn't play
> the song. Did he give up? NO!! He asked Mrs.
> Wilson if he could try again. Mrs. Wilson said
> he could come in after school, spend some
> time practising and then she would test him.
> HE MADE THE SCHOOL BAND!!! Mrs. Wilson is
> just one of those people who instinctively
> knows how to bring out the best in a student,
> knows how to make them work hard to
> achieve a success or a talent and the student
> is so motivated by her that they don't even
> realize how hard they have worked.

Re: Joseph Tersigni, a high school history teacher and national
conference organizer:

> This type of effort puts his students in a
> different world. They are not learning from a
> book but are in fact living the education
> because they are becoming directly involved in
> the issues.

Re: David Connolly, an experienced elementary teacher:

> I have found very few teachers that can
> compare to Mr. Connolly's teaching ability,

attitude and general generosity. I miss his camaraderie with his students, his sense of humor, even his rotten jokes, and his openness and fairness to all. Some may say that a year couldn't have made a difference to this degree in a person. A year made all the difference and more. Thanks Mr. C. In my eyes you are Teacher of the Year every year.

Re: Cheryl Upfold, who came to teaching in mid-life, after staying home to raise her own children:

If only we had a duplicating machine for humans ... we could put a Cheryl Upfold into every school in Canada and we'd have the best education system in the world.

Mrs. Upfold carries this nomination with such grace and poise. I am humbled to have made her happiness this great. Everyone connected to her is absolutely elated that such a fine educator has been recognized for her outstanding commitment to the lives of the children in her class.

I would like to tell you about one of the wonderful ways Mrs. Upfold has touched every single student at our school. When you first enter the lobby you can see hundreds of paper "cowboy boots" hanging from the ceiling. Each of these has a picture of a child in the school. On the reverse each child has written about what is most important about him or her. No one is left out and each child is recognized for their own unique abilities. This in a nutshell speaks volumes about the calibre of teacher Cheryl Upfold is. This was her own idea and it is hugely successful. Her ideas are fresh and innovative and touch the lives of those around her, whether it is a student, a fellow staff member or a parent. She is very much loved.

Re: Donald Martin, a principal in northern Ontario:

> The school spirit at our school is second to
> none, because of Mr. Martin's drive and
> energy. He seems to be on call 24 hours a day
> for our school. If you need to get into the
> school for something or another on a weekend
> or holiday, just call him at home. Some of our
> students often leave for school trips 5 or 6
> o'clock in the morning and you will find Mr.
> Martin at the school to make sure that every-
> thing is OK. If they arrive back at 11 that
> night, he is there again to make sure they all
> have a ride home.

Such are the educators who set the standards for the profession, standards that require a good teacher to be flexible, interesting, available, informed, accountable and relevant.

But beyond any single standard lies the complexity of the learning process and the relationship between learner and teacher. Together they will succeed or fail. Alone, teaching may take place but its effect on the student will fall short of learning.

One author of this book first came across a truly great teacher a long time ago while in secondary school. Before team teaching, independent study methods, group projects or technological aids of infinite variety arrived in the schools, he had a history teacher in a large urban high school who had honed the Socratic method of question and response to a fine art.

The teacher, J. Evan Cruickshank, was an instructional genius. He would introduce the lesson quickly and cogently, then begin asking a series of questions that had nothing to do with discovering whether homework had been done, or with lining up essential factual information such as names, dates and actions.

Rather, it was a profound exploration of the human motivations, the morality, the expectations and the consequences of the historical pageant. Even more, the flow of discussion between student and teacher, student and student not only exposed clearly a given sequence of events, but brought out its relevance to the present day.

After the traditional class time of forty minutes, his students realized that they had participated in a process that had provided them with an understanding of, and an excitement about, a far-off event, whether it was the American Revolution or Civil War, the signing of the British North America Act or the First Great War. Suddenly, the affairs of another generation were relevant and gave insights into current news. Most of those students had experienced a revelation, a transformation in their learning about the past.

A few weeks in that classroom, and the next generation of history teachers, including this author, had heard the call. Indeed, after studying with that one remarkable teacher in one secondary school, a number of students responded with pride and passion to his professional enthusiasm.

This whole book is based on mentors of such excellence. Not that the success of teachers should be judged on the basis of how many of their students follow in their professional footsteps. Rather, the standards explored in this volume speak to the total improvement of a population in its capacity to think clearly, express itself cogently, act generously with focus and force, thereby creating an educated community able to be productive, law-abiding and imaginative.

In this respect, modelling or teaching by example is critical. Teacher of the Year Larry Chiovitti is an excellent case in point. After high school, Larry Chiovitti decided to take a factory job and think about his future.

That future was decided for him when he went, two years later, to visit and help out in his cousin's classroom. He knew then and there that he wanted to be a teacher.

Two months later, Larry Chiovitti enrolled in teacher training and he has happily remained on the front line of elementary education ever since.

Larry Chiovitti was nominated by his current principal, who wrote:

> My nomination for Teacher of the Year is a co-staff member, who has been a regular class-room teacher for over twenty-five years.
> During this period he has fulfilled all the typical and non-typical roles that excellent teachers do without seeking recognition or fanfare. He is a lover of science and the scientific method and his pupils are exposed to a

great variety of actual experimentation far beyond normal expectations. His manner with pupils is fair and many families in the school look forward to the year when their sons and daughters will be in his classroom. He also works with pupils before and after school coaching sports and making sure assignments are completed by non-motivated pupils. I myself have been an educator for over twenty-five years. I have never witnessed such prolonged intensity and dedication related to regular classroom work.

The future is uncertain at best, depressing at worst. Only the finest preparation can work to our mutual benefit. However, in this world recession, education has been pinned to the wall. In Third World countries, the last decades have seen expenditures on education erode. Even in the richest countries, public expenditures on schools, colleges and universities have been seriously curbed.

The irony is obvious. At a time when all the rhetoric extols lifelong education for every citizen, public priorities dictate expenditures in other fields. Teachers find themselves facing new meanings for the word "knowledge" with expectations of horizontal, interdisciplinary connections in place of former understandings at the same time as many of the professional support systems are being pulled away, whether they be academic renewal, access to consultants, expanded resources or increased preparation time.

To influence the next generation is a powerful purpose of teaching. By lesson, by recommendation, by example, the teacher has the opportunity to be the greatest trendsetter of them all.

Teacher of the Year June Huyck is a superb example of the impact of such an influence. Her mother predicted that in order to graduate from high school, June would need to marry her teacher. Well, June did eventually marry one of her teachers. And she did ultimately graduate.

June Huyck left school after Grade 12 and worked as a secretary for three years before returning to complete Grade 13 at the age of twenty-one. That was when she met her future husband, her guidance teacher.

She then went to teachers' college and worked for several years, first as a teaching assistant and then as a school secretary, all the time coaching both boys' and girls' basketball and working on her university degree.

When her university degree was completed, Huyck began to teach math and special education at the school where she had first worked as a paraprofessional.

June has now been working for the same school board for twenty years and her background makes her uniquely qualified for her current post in adult education. Her students range in age from twenty-one to sixty-one, and they have returned to school after absences of up to forty years. The students, like their teacher, have faced failure, conquered school problems, and managed to reverse the drop-out syndrome.

June was nominated by one of her students who organized the full support of the student body. Here is what they wrote:

> We are a group of adult students returning to school to get our high school diplomas, or to learn new job skills, a daunting task after years in the work force. We came to the Lifetime Learning Centre, in nervous anticipation with some anxiety over our abilities. We feel that one of our instructors here is an especially outstanding teacher, and so we nominate June Huyck as Teacher of the Year.
>
> June is a source of daily inspiration to her students. Her commitment to help us succeed goes far beyond teaching just the required course of study. June has a truly remarkable knack for detecting any student who gets "lost" in a problem, and takes whatever time is needed to clear up any confusion. A particularly difficult matter will be approached from several angles, until the right avenue for that particular student is found. No student has ever been belittled, ignored, or put off, no matter what his/her level of achievement. Each one of us is treated with genuine respect. Daily, June displays wonderful patience and a droll sense of humor, when

dealing with a chaotic mix of many ages, different personalities and a broad range of academic backgrounds. She reminds us that she, also, left school and returned, several times as a matter of fact. She teaches, by example, that education is a lifelong experience, and that once we eliminate our fear of failure or success, we can choose to accomplish anything.

June's enthusiasm, warmth and positive outlook are contagious. She has shown us that each of us can make a difference in society. It is due to her constant encouragement and unfailing support that we complete this term having grown in ways we could not have imagined last September.

Unfortunately, most often teachers become too involved in following the ways of others to set the pace or determine the agenda. As new educational approaches evolve, as untried methods proliferate, as critics are heard, as budgets shrink, teachers lose more and more of their capacity to lead and, to the detriment of most, become scattered, divided followers.

Take the issue of standardized testing. Teachers as a group recognize the limitations of formal assessment. Too much time and money are spent on too little information about too few. And yet teachers toe the line and administer the tests.

Just as there is no formal assessment by testing that can yield the profile of the perfect teacher, there is no simple approach to understanding the magic of effective learning. A test provides only a snapshot of the determined specific. To do more demands standards of excellence.

The term "standards" as used in this book may be misleading. Rather than an objective measure, the word is used to indicate beacons, or symbols, just as the particular teachers we have described are symbols of success.

These standards are set forth to light the way for a profession now in one of its darkest hours. With criticism at a peak in a time of ever-lengthening job descriptions, as each teacher tries desperately to be all things to all people, it is time to remember what teachers do best — they teach!

CHAPTER 9

Conclusions

As we write this volume, the public attitude is aggressively anti-teacher. The attitude is almost uniform, and it is difficult to find defenders of our cause. Rather, we are beset with books, editorials, speeches, programs and political platforms voicing the same negative view. Teacher-bashing now fuels every forum on education.

The public outcry is understandable. When the economy deteriorates, scapegoats must be found. In this case the weakening of the economy must rest somewhat on the inadequacy of the schools. Ironically, the argument is never made that the previous boom may well have been the result of high quality in the classroom.

And what easy targets teachers are! Is it not obvious that teachers have security beyond most people's dreams, have lengthy holidays in the summer, at Christmas and in March and are paid a healthy salary to enjoy all these benefits? Rarely is there any coverage of the pressure of twelve-hour days of teaching, coaching, preparation and marking, and all in the face of a thousand critics. After all, everyone has gone to school, so everyone knows about education.

Strangely, most of the fury directed at teachers is in the collective — that is, the profession itself is under fire, but on the whole, parents are sympathetic to the teachers of their own children. Perhaps it is the realization of just how hard it is to keep their children occupied all day that enables them to appreciate the contribution of the individual classroom teacher.

Nevertheless, teachers today often feel abandoned, victims of a host of forces, facing constant harassment from the public, the administration, the media, the government — the list is endless.

The Teacher of the Year Award has sought to reverse this current. It began with an assumption, outlined in a weekly column on education in a large metropolitan newspaper, that there were many teachers doing a fine job. It came from casual discussion and personal experience; we all have memories of a teacher who made a difference in our lives.

The result was a call for nominations and a response that was overwhelming. Thousands of teachers have been put forward as deserving. Indeed the winners of the award came to be seen as representatives of a phalanx of excellent teachers in classrooms within reach of the newspaper's circulation. Our initial assumption was right. There are many standard bearers, splendid teachers who receive little or no attention.

At the extreme, some successful teachers never even meet their students yet achieve admirable standards of teaching excellence. For example, teachers of correspondence courses may make a critical difference to the lives of others, enriching job possibilities and lifestyle with virtually no direct contact or recognition. The following letter best exemplifies such an unsung hero:

> This unique teacher wins my Teacher of the Year Award. He's none other than Eric Robins of Oshawa. He helped me finish a nightmare and start a dream.
>
> Having failed Grade 12 Math in high school (a subject as clear as mud to me) I've had a feeling of inadequacy and leaving loose ends hanging, even though I graduated from Grade 13 and attended college. Most interesting jobs require Grade 12 Math and the new direction I wish to pursue is no exception.
>
> After calling the Independent Learning Centre to make the big step I was assigned to Eric Robins to complete my Math through correspondence. Through the mail he welcomed me to the world of numbers. He wrote at the start what he expected from me. He graded my papers carefully and explicitly and returned the lessons quickly. His compliments and praises were right at the top of the

page, a pat on the back. When I made a
mistake he called it a flaw (less drastic so the
fear didn't build) and showed me step by step
the correct solutions. He patiently answered
many questions. His encouraging words
helped push me through the middle lessons to
reach the end. It was he and I versus the Big
M. His enthusiastic support preceding the
final exam was reassuring. It was nice to
know someone believed in me. In the end we
conquered all. Without his encouragement I
know I would have given up half-way
through. To a man I've never met... Thank
you Eric! Thanks for believing in me!

Teaching can be a lonely job. Even colleagues do not often see
each others' outstanding lessons. Certainly they are unlikely to
feel the full impact of a teacher on a group of children they may
never meet. The relationship between teacher and parent is a
precious one, a bit like the confessional, but it is rarely truly col-
laborative. Often it is not until retirement that any fuss is made
of a person who may have served a community and its children
for decades.

Perhaps the ultimate irony is that the only way a teacher can
achieve promotion is to leave the classroom and become an
administrator or consultant. This process leads to the most
erroneous conclusion of all, that the classroom teacher is at the
bottom of the pyramid and that the brightest and the best have
gone on to more important things. The idea that a professional
would choose to stay in the classroom with less compensation
and recognition seems to be out of tune with modern values —
and yet many excellent teachers take this path.

There are many lessons to be gained from the winners of these
teaching awards. The variety of philosophies, characters, styles
and performance is obvious and shows that there is no pattern
to be followed slavishly, only certain strengths to be taken into
account. Indeed, there is no perfect teacher for every student,
rather differences in both that will lead either to a perfect match
or, in extreme cases, an ugly confrontation.

The teachers described in this book do, however, have much
in common. Each one has a well-defined philosophy of educa-

tion that emerges from a reflective nature. They know what they are doing, what they have done. They are aware of the outcomes they wish to achieve and can judge when they have succeeded and when they have failed. They are competent; they are confident.

In fact, a recipe for success in teaching would dictate equal doses of competence and confidence; an imbalance would defeat our goals.

Once the ratio of competence and confidence is secure, a teacher can concentrate on the only meaningful focus, the potential of each student. While it is clear that any number of circumstances may make learning difficult, even impossible on occasion, the good teacher never wavers in his or her complete respect for each child's ability to learn.

Many students come to school hungry. They may be victims of violence in the home, the street or playground. Even more likely, they are victims of vicarious violence they have seen on television. To be charitable, rather than dramatic, such children are not ready to learn. Yet good teachers have such faith in the attractiveness of learning that they believe that all can be overcome, that their reaching out will ultimately prevail over the apparent indifference and distaste that characterize many students' immediate reaction to their teachers' efforts.

The formal curriculum is merely a launching pad for adventure that goes far beyond the limitations of an official document. Drawing on an immense store of information and experience, teachers can create an environment in which curiosity is excited and fulfilled.

In the minds of the Teachers of the Year, the school is but a passing phase in a lifetime of learning that must envelop both teacher and student. Lifelong learning has moved from the fringe to the very centre of our consciousness in just a few years. There has always been a progressive coterie of adult educators, led for decades by J. Roby Kidd, who preached the gospel of continuing education. Now lifelong learning is an oft-repeated slogan of every level of government. Success depends on the understanding of teachers and students that both are engaged in enhancing a fragment of a learning life. No longer is it enough to fill a bag with information. Rather, learning is about skills and learning how to learn. It is about literacy, in languages, in mathematics, in science, in history, in economics and in the arts.

These teachers of our time have each sensed the nature of the future, feel comfortable with that future and can guide their students to an understanding of the world they will face.

The quality of these teachers and those they represent raises questions about the governance of our schools. As this book is being written, there are moves across the country which may result in the reduction in numbers of boards of education, an erosion in the size of each and serious limitations on their power.

And yet there is a growing distrust of large bureaucracies, a sense that the basic decisions about learning should take place at the local level, with appropriate input from the community. Our study of winning teachers confirms that approach with the simple fact of front-line competence. After all, a decentralized system of education will ultimately rest on the intelligence and the commitment of the classroom teacher. Decisions about curriculum, skills development and coping with individual differences may be best responded to at the school level, where there can be effective cooperation by parents and other interested citizens.

Perhaps of all the attributes that surfaced as common among all the very different people who were selected as Teachers of the Year the most important was that of caring, a deep concern for the total well-being of the students, the way each child learns, the way each child feels, the way each child develops. And this sensitivity was the characteristic most often identified by parents, students and even colleagues in their nominations.

Because of this caring, the teachers showed a willingness to start where the student was to be found at the point of contact. These teachers possessed the determination to take each student as far as possible in the time available. Everyone perceived this willingness as an awareness of all the forces which both encourage and inhibit learning.

Every child will, at some point, be inspired by a great teacher. However, between great teachers, each educational life will be influenced by many good, intelligent, thoughtful teachers.

But one prays that every teacher who comes in contact with every child will care, and care deeply. It is not too much to ask.

In Your Hands

(Song for my Teacher)

Teacher, I wrote this song for you
To thank you for every smile.
I know you had a lot to do,
I'm glad that you paused a while.

You took time to listen, and to hear,
To laugh, and just be there;
I heard that lesson loud and clear:
I mattered to you — you cared.

CHORUS:
'cause

When you reach out, and you touch me with your heart,
Then you hold what I'm becoming in your hands,
And though you're with me just a while
Today you hold tomorrow's smile
In your hands... In your hands... In your hands.

Teacher, I wrote this song for you:
Melody, words and rhyme.
Lessons you taught me yesterday
Have disappeared into time.

But, teacher, I never will forget
A look you gave to me;
I saw reflected in your eyes
The somebody I could be.

Written by recording artist and educator Ron Hiller (Ronno) and his sister Judy Miller in memory of their special teachers and as a tribute to today's caring teachers, who can make a profound difference in their students' lives.